Serving the King

Serving the King

a guide to Christian usefulness

Derek Thomas

 EVANGELICAL PRESS

EVANGELICAL PRESS
12 Wooler Street, Darlington, County Durham, DL1 1RQ, England.

© Evangelical Press 1989
First published 1989

ISBN 0 85234 270 5

Unless otherwise stated, all Scripture quotations are taken from the
New King James Version, © 1984, Thomas Nelson, Inc.

Printed in Great Britain by Cox and Wyman, Reading.

To
Madge and Anna Speers
for showing me what Christian
service is

Contents

Preface

As Christians, we are to serve our Master. The Lord has something for each of us to do for him. Learning what our special task for God is can be both frustrating and rewarding at the same time. Frustrating, because the process of learning it is hardly ever as straightforward as we imagine. Rewarding, because there is nothing in this life more pleasant than knowing we are doing our Father's will.

'Every-member ministry' has become a slogan in some circles, sometimes to pour scorn over traditional views of office and ministry in the church. I have no desire in these pages to enter into this controversy, except, as will become evident, to defend by way of an assumption throughout, that God calls some men into special offices (preachers, elders, deacons etc.). Rather, my concern is to focus our thoughts upon the need for every one of us to be busy for Christ.

There are, I suppose, two ways of going about this task. One could approach it in a systematic way, drawing together what the Bible has to say about service. Although I have done a little of that in the first chapter, my approach, on the whole, has been different. I have instead taken the biographical details of several individuals in Scripture to illustrate examples of usefulness in the service of God.

Following an initial chapter outlining why every Christian

should be involved in service, two chapters follow dealing with guidance. Chapter 2 takes the example of Paul and the way he was led into serving Christ in Europe. Guidance is one of those areas where Christians experience considerable difficulty. One such difficulty occurs when we experience problems. If I am led into this or that particular service, and problems arise, can I be sure that I am still walking in God's will? Chapter 3 takes up this issue, taking Joseph as our example.

No one can be really useful for God whose life does not reflect something of him. Holiness is essential to witness; holiness is *itself* witness! Being different for God is the theme of the fourth chapter.

I have included two chapters dealing with particular problems that some of God's servants face: coping with immaturity (Chapter 5: Timothy is our example here), and depression (Chapter 6, taking a trio of Old Testament workers: Jeremiah, Elijah and Jonah).

The parable of the talents (Matt. 25:14-30) teaches a very important truth: some Christians are more gifted than others, though not necessarily more useful. The Lord takes special care of those who are less gifted (1 Cor. 12:23). I have, therefore, included two chapters illustrating one who had great gifts (Ezra) and one with lesser gifts (Mary of Bethany). Both, in their own way, served the Lord well.

Finally, I have sought to end this short study by taking the example of Joseph of Arimathea, a man whose usefulness only becomes apparent in one deed. Joseph of Arimathea is a challenge to us. Undoubtedly we should learn the negative lesson that our discipleship should not be secretive and retiring as his was. But, there is something positive too. God has chosen some of us to do one great deed for him. Discovering what that may be, and doing it to his glory is to be our aim in this life.

Go, labour on: spend and be spent,
Thy joy to do the Father's will;
It is the way the Master went;
Should not the servant tread it still?

These words by Horatius Bonar sum up almost everything I
want to say in this book, though not everything there is to say
about service is contained in these pages! It is the longing of
my heart that what is said here may both enlighten and spur on
to new areas of Christian service those who read. We need to
catch a glimpse of the glory of our great God 'to whom we
belong and whom we serve' (cf.Acts 27:23). If that is accomplished, even in some small measure, my objective has been
met.

I am indebted to Ernest Brown for his tireless efforts in
reading this manuscript and for his many helpful suggestions.
I am also grateful to Evangelical Press for agreeing to publish
it.

Derek Thomas
Belfast

1.
Called to usefulness

I must confess to being something of a hoarder. All kinds of things, from boxes to jiffy bags, are put away in the vague notion that one day 'they might come in useful'. They hardly ever do; just at the time when I need them I can never find them.

Most Christians, in times of heightened spiritual awareness, have a longing to be useful for God. They have felt the need to say with Isaiah, 'Here am I! Send me' (Isa. 6:8). Sometimes it is identified as a call to the ministry or the mission field. After all, our ideas of useful Christians are the lives of the great giants of the faith: Reformers like John Calvin, Thomas Cranmer, or John Knox; preachers like George Whitefield, John Wesley or Daniel Rowlands; or missionaries like Hudson Taylor, William Carey or Jim Elliot.

Most of us are awed by the usefulness of the shy, diffident John Calvin who wanted nothing more than to be a lifelong student, reading and writing books. But it was not to be: Guillaume Farel, whose fierce, red-bearded face would have terrified anyone, threatened the curse of God upon him if he did not stay in Geneva and become a pastor.

Calvin slept only four hours in the night, preached lengthy expository sermons almost every day, and toiled away at his writing producing one of the finest classics of Christian literature which remains the single, most influential commentary upon Christian doctrine today, *The Institutes of the Christian Religion*. Add to that a series of commentaries on the books of the Bible (running, at least in my own edition, to over 11,000 pages) and you will understand why the man suffered from fevers, ulcers, haemorrhaging from various parts of the body, gall-stones and piles. Writing to Bullinger on 6 April 1564 he had this to say: 'Although the pain in my side is abated, my lungs are so full of phlegm that my breathing is difficult and short. A stone in my bladder has been very troublesome for the last twelve days...Horse riding would have been best, but an ulcer in the haemorrhoid veins tortures me even when sitting down or lying in bed, so that I could not bear the agitation of riding. Within the last days the gout has also been very troublesome. You will not be surprised, then, if so many sufferings make me lazy.'[1] In his later life he was weakened by increasing pulmonary tuberculosis and eventually he died at the age of fifty-five, burnt-out. Now, that's usefulness.

Or take John Wesley. It is said that Wesley travelled some 250,000 miles on horseback and preached on 40,000 occasions. Most of his reading, sermon preparation, and considerable literary output were done on the back of a horse! Typical of his diary entries are the following:

Mon. 2: I preached at five [i.e. in the morning] and rode on towards Cornwall. The hills were covered with snow, as in the depth of winter. About two we came to Trewint, wet and weary enough, having been battered by the rain and hail for some hours. I preached in the evening, to many more than the house would contain, on the happiness of him whose sins are forgiven. In the morning [a granite mason] undertook to pilot me over the great moor, the paths being covered with snow which in many places was driven together too deep for horse or man to pass. The hail followed us for the first seven miles; we then had a fair though exceedingly sharp day. I preached at Gwennap in the evening to a plain, simple-hearted people; and God comforted us by each other.

Wed. 4 :About eleven we reached St Ives...As soon as we went out we were saluted, as usual, with a huzza [hurrah] and a few stones or pieces of dirt.[2]

Wesley, too, was one of God's useful servants.

Or take Jim Elliot, missionary to Ecuador and the Peruvian Indians of the Andes. His murder by the Auca Indians some thirty years ago, retold in the two books *Through Gates of Splendour* and *Shadow of the Almighty* is one of the most moving tales in missionary biographies. One of his diary entries recalls what the lack of usefulness meant to him:

July 21: Felt condemned yesterday by the Word as I sat down to meditate at the Lord's Supper. 'I will not offer any of that which cost me nothing to the Lord,' said David (2 Sam. 24:24). I realized that I had paid out nothing last week to really get something to offer the Lord. So as I confessed my sin, the Lord forgave and began to feed my meditation from the Gospels with thoughts of the patience of the Lamb. [3]

Jim Elliot was another of God's useful servants. What does it mean to be useful for God? It is the question that we shall seek to answer in this book.

First things first!

Since we shall be dealing with the place of service in the Christian life we need to get some things straight right at the very start. No one can be made right with God on account of his works. We are saved by grace, the unmerited favour of God (Eph. 2:8-9).

Every religion apart from evangelical Christianity has the same basic flaw: each rings the changes on self-salvation. Being saved is construed as something we do; redemption is God's reward for a work well done, a payment given for services rendered. The Bible insists that it is otherwise, for as the Reformers so eloquently expressed it, salvation is by faith *alone* without any obligation to work for it; it is by grace *alone* without any sense of earning it; it is by Christ *alone* without there being any need or room for any other mediatorial agent (priest, saint or virgin); it is by Scripture *alone*, there being no other ground of authority; and all the glory must be given to God *alone*, there being no place for self-congratulation.

But if entry into the kingdom is without works on our part, the evidence of entry is a life filled with service: 'We are his workmanship, created in Christ Jesus for good works'(Eph. 2:10). A trilogy of exhortations in the pastoral epistles makes the point clear. Christians are to be *rich in good works* (1 Tim. 6:18). The Lord has given us the Scriptures, his inerrant Word, *to equip us for every good work* (2 Tim. 3:17). Members of God's kingdom are to be *zealous for good works* (Titus 2:14). As David Wenham has put it: 'There is truth in the old saying that the entry fee to Christianity is completely free, but the annual subscription is everything we've got.'[4]

Every - member ministry

Whenever we think about Christian service we usually think of the 'ministry'. Consequently, we also tend to think that when God calls us into his service it will be with a special kind of call. After all, special usefulness does demand a special call. Think of Samuel; his call was special (1 Sam. 3:1-10). God spoke to him directly — more than once! He was a prophet, priest and the last of the judges all at the same time. His office was special, and so was his call. The same is true of men like Moses (Exod. 3:4-22), Isaiah (Isa. 6:1-8), Jeremiah (Jer. 1:4-

12) and Paul (Acts 9:1-19). In every case, God had a special ministry for them to perform. He made each one of them aware of it in a very special and dramatic way.

The way God calls a man into the Christian ministry today is quite different. To begin with, he no longer speaks directly as he did in Bible times. Now that we have his Word written down in the Bible, God 'speaks' in a different way. Nevertheless, it remains true that since the ministry is a 'special' work, so too is God's calling.

Four factors outline a call to the ministry:

1. Any calling to a special ministry is *a call from God.* When men after God's own heart are needed for ministry the Lord himself seeks them out. We see this in the life of David: three times the Bible tells us that the Lord sought and found him (1 Sam. 13:14; Ps. 89:20; Acts 13:22). Those who give their lives 'continually to prayer and to the ministry of the word' (Acts 6:4) must have a heart patterned after God's own heart; and only God can discern such. Those in special service need the Lord to say, 'Arise, anoint him; for this is the one!' (1 Sam. 16:12). Or, 'Separate to me Barnabas and Saul for the work to which I have called them' (Acts 13:2).

2. How will we know when God is calling us? Along with God's call, there is given *a desire for the work* (cf.1 Tim. 3:1). This desire must not be confused with the presence of reticence. Moses, Isaiah and Jeremiah made all kinds of excuses, but each had a call. Spurgeon said that 'The first sign of the heavenly calling is an intense, all-absorbing desire for the work.'[5]

3. There must be the necessary *gifts and graces* (cf. 1 Tim. 3:1-7). God calls no man into the ministry whom he does not first equip for the task. These gifts and graces may only be evidenced in embryo, but they must be present.

4. There must be *a recognition of the call;* God makes his wisdom known *through the church* (Eph. 3:10). Far too often this principle is ignored. If God wants a man in the ministry he will make sure that others will see it too! Sometimes others will recognize evidences of God's call before we are even aware of it. This was true in the case of John Knox. It was John Rough who pointed out to Knox, during his time at the Protestant garrison of St Andrews, that he believed he was called for special service. Even though Knox couldn't see it himself, and fought the notion for several days, eventually he came to see that he had been chosen to be 'the Trumpeter of God'.

These four factors will help a man to see whether or not God has called him into the ministry. We need to appreciate, however, that *everyone* is called into service for God.

Every Christian has something to do for God. There are no useless Christians in his kingdom. The Sermon on the Mount makes clear that Christ expects from every believer the highest standards of service. Every 'blessed' man will live in such a way as to be the salt of the earth and the light of the world (Matt. 5:13-16). It is the same in Paul's letters. The idea of a Christian unfit for service is absurd! Christians who have been redeemed from sin have become servants of righteousness (Rom. 6:18). Peter also makes the same point: 'But you are a chosen generation, a royal priesthood, a holy nation, his own special people, that you may proclaim the praises of him who called you out of darkness into his marvellous light' (1 Peter 2:9).

The passage from 1 Peter is an example of 'every-member ministry'. It makes clear that witness-bearing is a task expected of every Christian. We are all to evangelize. Each one is charged with holding fast his profession (Heb. 4:14), holding fast the word of life (Phil. 2:16), giving a reason for the hope within him (1 Peter 3:15).

The early church saw this principle clearly. Following the persecution that had broken out in Jerusalem after the death of Stephen, we are told that the Christians 'all scattered throughout the regions of Judea and Samaria, except the apostles'. A few verses later we are informed that 'those who were scattered went everywhere preaching the word' (Acts 8:1-4). This was in fulfilment of Jesus' resurrection promise, 'But you shall receive power when the Holy Spirit has come upon you; and you shall be witnesses to me in Jerusalem, and in all Judea and Samaria, and to the end of the earth' (Acts 1:8). The word Luke uses in Acts 8:4 translated 'preaching' is the word *euanggelizomai* (the verb form of the noun 'evangel' or 'gospel'). Christians who left Jerusalem for fear of persecution went and 'gospelled' the gospel elsewhere. Every Christian saw evangelism as his calling.

Eyes, hands, feet and ears

It is vital for us to see that every member of Christ's body has an important role to play. Paul takes up two whole chapters to make this very point (Rom. 12; 1 Cor. 12). To the surprise of the very gifted brethren in Corinth who were in danger of using their special endowments as an occasion for pride and one-upmanship, Paul insists that every believer is baptized in the Spirit, and thereby equipped for service. It is by means of Holy Spirit baptism (conversion) that we become members of his body (1 Cor. 12:13). No one can say, 'Jesus is Lord' except 'by the Holy Spirit' (v.3). We all drink from the same Spirit. Each one is gifted in a different way: using the analogy of the body he makes reference to eyes, hands, feet and ears (vv. 15-17). The purpose of these gifts is not to produce freelance, independent Christians. Rather, they are 'for the profit of all' (v.7).

Some Christians feel themselves *inferior*. 'If the foot should say, "Because I am not a hand, I am not of the body," is it therefore not of the body?' (v.15). A housewife with an endless cycle of meals to prepare and children's clothes to wash and iron may feel inferior. She is not! The eye is as important as the ear (v.17).

Some Christians feel *superior*. They are tempted to look down at others and sneer. 'I have no need of you,' they say. They are too big for their boots. They need to learn that every member of the body is necessary (v. 22). In fact, God takes special care of those who appear less gifted! (v. 23). Just think, for example, how protective a mother can be over one of her children less confident, less able than her other children. I remember being introduced to a family of several children where one had Down's Syndrome. 'And this is our special son,' his mother said with obvious sincerity.

The ascended Christ distributes his gifts to the church's members (Eph. 4:7-8) and thus 'every-member ministry' is expected in the church's life. Not all members are preachers, or elders, or deacons, or Sunday school teachers. The multifaceted wisdom of God is seen in the distribution of gifts in the church: 'As each one has received a gift, minister it to one another, as good stewards of the manifold grace of God' (1 Peter 4:10). Growth and maturity of the body depends upon every member appreciating this very point: 'Every part does its share' (Eph. 4:16).

A trilogy of parables

That every Christian is expected to perform a work of usefulness is also underlined in some of the many parables of Jesus. There are in fact about a hundred references in the four Gospels to parables, though about half this number are repetitions of the same parable. It is true to say, however, that Jesus' ministry was full of parables: short pithy sayings designed as sermon illustrations (much like their Old Testament equivalent in the book of Proverbs).

   Three parables in particular emphasize 'every-member ministry'.

The parable of the talents (Matt. 25:14-30) is one of many parables involving a master going on a journey. The master goes away leaving his vast wealth in the hands of his employees. Different servants are given five, two and one talent each respectively to use wisely for their master in his absence. A talent was roughly the equivalent of ten years' wages, what might amount to £100,000 today! Thus five talents would be in the region of half a million pounds! The master entrusts an amount to them 'each according to his own ability' (v.15, cf. 'to each his work' in the parable of the watchmen, Mark 13:34). Every one is entrusted with some of the Lord's resources. In this way the parable reflects vividly the teaching of Romans 12 and 1 Corinthians 12 where we are told that the body has many members.

   Of particular note is the charge brought against the servant who merely dug a hole and buried his talent, thereby producing nothing to give to his master. He is called 'wicked and lazy' (v. 26). He is in effect useless. His talent is taken away and he himself thrown into 'outer darkness'. Like the man who hid his light when it was needed (Matt. 5:15), this servant is of no use in the Master's service.

   Christians who don't produce fruit are not genuine Christians at all. Being co-workers together with Christ is a test of our genuineness.

The parable of the minas (Luke 19:11-27) is very similar to that of the talents. In almost every detail it is identical except that each one receives the same amount, one mina (roughly equivalent to three months' wages). This time the nobleman goes away in order to get a kingdom for himself. Citizens try in vain to prevent this nobleman from becoming king, but fail and are punished with death. The difference in emphasis reflects another truth that we have already seen: whereas Matthew's parable stresses the point that each member has different gifts (cf.1 Cor.12:20), Luke's parable makes the point that every Christian in God's kingdom is equal before God, despite the variety of gifts (1 Cor. 12:13).

In this parable also the servant who wraps up his amount in a handkerchief for safe-keeping, producing nothing to give to his master when he returns, is described as 'wicked' (Luke 19:22). The mina he received is taken away from him and given to the others. Again, service is a test of our genuineness.

The parable of the humble servant (Luke 17:7-10) makes yet another point: service is not to be rendered for reward's sake. A man with a smallholding and just one servant sends him out to the field to work for the day. In the afternoon he returns. Should he sit down and put his feet up? Of course not! He must now set about preparing and serving the evening meal. When all this is done his master, who may well be grateful for such willing work rendered to him, has no cause for celebration. His servant has only done what is expected of him. In today's terms a man who works a forty-hour week should not expect an amount for overtime in his pay packet! At best we have only done what Christ has a right to expect of us. Like this servant, we too are purchased slaves for Christ. God expects all his children to serve him!

Five New Testament words

In 1 Corinthians 12:4-6 Paul uses three words in quick succession which help us appreciate what all this means. There are varieties of gifts (*charismata*), ministries, or service *(diakonia)* and activities *(energemata)*.

Contrary to current views on the subject, every Christian is a charismatic. This does not mean that we are to expect the extraordinary sign-gifts (tongues, prophecy, word of knowledge etc.) today. These were signs of the apostles (2 Cor. 12:12) which ceased with them. But other gifts remain: wisdom, knowledge, teaching, counselling, government, leadership, serving, comforting, exhorting, liberality, administration. The Christian widow who puts her mite into the offering box is no less charismatic than the Corinthian tongue-speaker. Both have received Holy Spirit baptism; both perform their task by the Holy Spirit's help.[6]

There are also various ministries (*diakonia*). This is the most common word for ministry in the New Testament. It is from this word we get our English word 'deacon'. Timothy's and Erastus' ministry to Paul during his time at Ephesus (which no doubt involved writing down his letters and cooking his meals) is referred to as diaconal work (Acts 19:22), as is prison-visiting (Philem. 13) and evangelistic preaching (Acts 20:24). So, too, is the work of a godly woman called Phoebe in Cenchrea (Rom.16:1). That there is a special office of deacon does not detract from the fact that every member of the church has diaconal functions to perform. The church needs preachers, elders and deacons. But it also needs Sunday school teachers and youth leaders. It needs far more to function usefully. It needs those like Barnabas who are gifted with a warm, welcoming spirit, able to encourage the church into corporate action for Christ (cf. Acts 11:23; 13:43). It needs the ministry of older women to give counsel and example to the younger women of the congregation (Titus 2:4). It needs skilled labourers who are able to care for the fabric of ageing church buildings, and much, much more.

There are also various activities (*energemata*), a word which suggests the *energy* of the Holy Spirit necessary for the carrying out of even the smallest of tasks. In its verb form it is used as a description of the power at work in the ministry of Jesus, which led some to think he was John the Baptist risen from the dead (Matt. 14:2; Mark 6:14).

If these three words suggest the variety of ministry in the church, two more New Testament words make it clearer.

The first is the word 'servant' or 'slave' *(doulos)*. Every Christian is a servant, or slave of Christ. Paul sometimes used it to describe his relation to his own converts (1 Cor. 9:19-23; 2 Cor. 4:5). Far from seeing himself as an overbearing superior, Paul put himself in the place of a lowly servant, reflecting the gesture of his Lord who came in 'the form of a servant' (Phil. 2:7), and in the upper room pictured it by washing the disciples' feet (John 13:1-5).

More often than not, however, Paul uses this word as a description of his relation to Christ (Rom.1:1, etc). As he faced imminent execution in a prison in Rome he alludes to wearing the chain of a slave (2 Tim. 1:16). Christians who have been redeemed from sin's bondage now yield themselves to Christ's yoke as the only fitting response: 'You are not your own,' he says, 'for you were bought at a price' (1 Cor. 6:19-20). Like Roman slaves they had no rights: everything about them — money, time, marriage, abilities — were their master's. Christians are slaves of Jesus Christ.

The other word describing Christian service is *leitourgos* from which we get our English word 'liturgy'. It is used of the worship of God by angels in heaven (Heb. 1:14) and men on earth (Luke 1:23). It is also used to describe the worship offered by the members of the church in Antioch as the Holy Spirit called upon them to separate Paul and Barnabas for even greater usefulness (Acts 13:2). In Hebrews it describes the 'ministry' of Christ in his atoning work, particularly as it fulfils various typical foreshadowings in the Old Testament (Heb. 8:2,6 etc.). In Romans 13 it describes those who carry out judicial sentences upon criminals: they are 'ministers of God' (v.6). Sacrificial giving is described this way (2 Cor. 9:12; Rom. 15:27), as is the service of Epaphras (Phil. 2:30) and Paul's preaching to the heathen (Rom. 15:16).

Worship is part of our Christian service! And clearly, every Christian is called to worship the Lord.

To summarize:

> *charismata* — lays stress on the gifts being gracious endowments of the Holy Spirit;
>
> *diakonia* — emphasizes the variety of tasks that can be done for the Lord;
>
> *energemata* — makes the point that every task rendered needs the aid of the Holy Spirit;
>
> *doulos* — shows us that service is to be offered in humble obedience as part of the duty God expects from us;
>
> *leitourgos* — reminds us that all service is part of our worship, the way we glorify him and enjoy him for ever.

What we have seen in these first few pages is that every Christian has a task to do for God. We shall need to know God's guidance if we are to learn what that task is. Guidance is the theme of the next chapter.

2.
Showing us the way

Every Christian needs to know what God expects by way of service. He needs to be shown the way. Muddled views on guidance bring confusion as to what our service should be. This is an area where Christians need to go back to their Bibles and learn afresh what God has taught about the way he leads his people.

A study of Acts 16:6-10, an example of the way God guided Paul, can help us here. In this passage we see an example of how God leads his servants into new areas of use-fulness. Paul was never idle, and even before the Holy Spirit changed the course of his service we notice that the apostle intended to serve the Lord. Two things in particular help us to see that, even before the Holy Spirit dramatically altered his course, the apostle knew what God expected of him. First, he had well-defined goals. He knew what he wanted to accomplish by God's help. Second, he recognized that the Lord gives gifts to others apart from himself. Godly fellow-labourers are a great asset in Christian work. Before God intervened to change the apostle's plans, he got on with the task in hand. That is something we too are always meant to be doing.

To Antioch

The apostle, together with some of the other leaders, had left
the Jerusalem Council and travelled northwards to Antioch
(Acts 15: 22). In Jerusalem they had reaffirmed their commitment to the gospel. No one can be made right with God by his
own works. A man is saved by turning away from his sin and
trusting in Jesus Christ alone. Various factions were trying to
say something different, and this was a battle the church had
to win; had they failed there would be no gospel to preach.
Jews who insisted upon the necessity for converted Gentiles to
be circumcised and obey the ceremonial laws of the Old Testament were contradicting the gospel.

Having returned to Antioch they spent some time in the
church in a ministry of 'strengthening' (Acts 15:32). After
some time had elapsed Paul decided that another journey was
in order, to visit the churches established on the first missionary journey (in Galatia and Cyprus), suggesting to Barnabas,
'Let us now go back and visit our brethren in every city where
we have preached the word of the Lord, and see how they are
doing' (Acts 15:36). Luke uses a word (translated 'visit', v.
36) which (in another form) is the word used for an 'elder' or
'bishop' or 'shepherd'. Later, Luke adds the comment that
Paul 'went through Syria and Cilicia, *strengthening* the
churches' (v.41), again using the same word as for his strengthening ministry in Antioch (v. 32). Paul was more than just a
preacher. He was a shepherd and an encourager! He *cared* for
the people to whom he ministered.

Paul had in mind a visit that would confirm and consoli-
date the work already begun. It was to be more than just a social
visit. He had clear objectives in mind. He had preached the
gospel, laying solid foundations. Now, he desired to see solid
structures established. Young converts needed to be taught the
things of God. They needed to be discipled in the ways of
godliness. In understanding they were to be men (1 Cor.
14:20). Christian workers who have no clear goals are in

serious trouble. Every now and then we need to stop and ask ourselves, 'What am I doing here?' and 'Where am I going?'

Paul's plans were changed by the Holy Spirit's leading. He was sent on from Galatia to Troas and over to Macedonia. Later, he was instrumental in planting churches in the capital cities of the three Roman provinces of Macedonia (with its capital at Thessalonica), Achaia (with its capital at Corinth) and Asia (with its capital at Ephesus). We need only think of what Paul would later say to these churches, in letters written to each one, to imagine what he had in mind for this visit to Cyprus and Galatia.

The Ephesians were taught such doctrines as predestination, depravity, the freeness of grace and the privileges of being a Christian, summed up in that magnificent prayer in Ephesians 3:14-19. And by way of practical application he exhorts godliness in marriage (5:22-33), the home (with children in mind, 6:1-4), and the place of work (6:5-9). In Paul's first letter to the church at Corinth, he gives instruction on such things as sexual immorality (1 Cor. 5), law-suits (1 Cor. 6), spiritual gifts (1 Cor. 12-14), and the doctrine of the resurrection (1 Cor. 15). And when he writes to the Thessalonians he has to give some instruction about the doctrine of the Second Coming of Christ (1 Thess. 4:13-18; 2 Thess. 2) and advice over such things as chastity (1 Thess. 4:3-8), and laziness (2 Thess. 3:6-15).

When Paul says he wished to 'visit' the churches we can have some idea what that meant! Paul had clear objectives in mind. A clear strategy is always necessary for a work to be done well. Can you write down some of the goals you have in mind for the work you are doing for God?

Godly fellow-labourers

Paul never worked alone. He always worked as part of a team. In that sense he was following the pattern of our Lord who

called twelve disciples and sent them out two by two (Mark
6:7). Later he sent them out in a group of seventy (Luke 10:1).

Paul had intended to take Barnabas with him on this
journey. It is hardly surprising! Who would not wish to have
the company of a man whose name means 'son of encouragement'? Barnabas was the kind of man who could cheer you up
when you felt discouraged. Maybe it was his happy, smiling
face. Maybe it was that ability to say the right thing at the right
time. Maybe it was the combination of godliness, ability,
wisdom and cheerfulness that made him such an asset.

However, it was not to be. Paul and Barnabas quarrelled
over John Mark! Luke spares nothing in the account. 'Then the
contention became so sharp that they parted from one another,' he comments (Acts 15:39). There can hardly be sadder
words in all the Scriptures relating to the behaviour of two
godly and respected men. The issue was simple enough. John
Mark had let them down on the first missionary journey by
deciding at Paphos to go back to Jerusalem (Acts 13:13). No
reason is given. It may be that he was a little put out that Paul
(and not his cousin, Barnabas) was given the limelight. Maybe
the journey was too difficult and the prospects worse. The fact
of the matter was that John Mark had not proved himself and
Paul was not for giving him a second chance. Barnabas was far
more conciliatory and wished him to go. Neither felt able to
compromise. It was a regrettable incident where compromise
was surely possible, but neither wished to surrender. A parting
was the only course left open. Barnabas took John Mark and
went to Cyprus.

Incidents like this one occur far too often in Christian
work. Disagreements amongst labourers for the gospel over
secondary matters are always regrettable. They are evidence
of the deep-seated sin that remains in us even when we are
redeemed and forgiven.

Instead of Barnabas, Paul took Silas, the leader of the
Jerusalem church and a prominent Jewish Christian who also
ministered to the Greek-speaking church at Antioch where he

is referred to as a prophet (Acts 15:22,32). He also had a Roman name, Silvanus (2 Cor. 1:19; 1 Thess. 1:1; 2 Thess. 1:1; 1 Peter 5:12) and Roman citizenship (Acts 16:37-39). It has been suggested that Silas had a function similar to that of Mark in looking after the Scriptures and scrolls. Peter credits Silas with a hand in the writing of his epistles (1 Peter 5:12). With such qualifications he was an ideal companion.

Timothy also went on this journey. He was to be a companion with Paul in his journeys for the next fifteen years. Having a Jewish mother and a Greek father gave him dual nationality and access into both Jewish and Gentile territories. There was, however, the matter of his circumcision (or rather, the lack of it). In order to have access to the Jews (that they might recognize him as one of them) Paul insisted that he undergo the procedure. There was no point of principle involved here as there was in Galatia (where the Judaizers were insisting that it was necessary in order to be saved, Gal. 2:1-3).

It is always good to have companions in gospel work. How important friends were to the apostle can be seen from 2 Timothy 4:9-22, some of the last words the apostle ever wrote. In this, his last letter, the apostle mentions several people who were close to him: Priscilla and Aquila (with whom he had stayed in Corinth, Acts 18:2), 'the household of Onesiphorus' (Onesiphorus himself was still separated from his family and in Rome, 2 Tim. 1:16-18), Erastus (the city treasurer of Corinth who accompanied Timothy into Macedonia, Rom. 16:23; Acts 19:22), Trophimus (who accompanied Paul to Jerusalem, Acts 20:1-5; 21:29), and the Roman Christians who probably visited Paul in prison, Eubulus, Pudens, Linus and Claudia. Then there were Crescens, Titus and Tychicus, the latter being described as 'a beloved brother and faithful minister...in the Lord'.

So important were friends to Paul that he bade Timothy (who was in Jerusalem) bring Mark with him even though, as we have seen, Mark had let him down earlier and been the cause of a major disagreement between the apostle and Barnabas

(2 Tim. 4:11). Above all Paul wanted to see Timothy who must come soon, before the onset of winter (2 Tim. 1:4).

Clearly, friends are important in gospel work! Speaking to his disciples, Jesus said, 'You are my friends...' (John 15:14).

Divine guidance

Acts 16 provides us with a fascinating example of guidance. If it is necessary for God's servants to have clear objectives and godly fellow-labourers, it is just as essential that they be guided. Luke provides us with the barest of details. 'Now when they had gone through Phrygia and the region of Galatia, they were forbidden by the Holy Spirit to preach the word in Asia. After they had come to Mysia, they tried to go into Bithynia, but the Spirit did not permit them. So passing by Mysia, they came down to Troas. And a vision appeared to Paul in the night. A man of Macedonia stood and pleaded with him, saying, "Come over to Macedonia and help us"' (Acts 16:6-9).

Their intended route had been south-west (towards the province of Asia and the capital at Ephesus) but they were prevented from doing so and had to turn northwards. They attempted to go towards Bithynia but were again prevented from doing so and were forced to turn north-west towards Troas. We are not told how it was that the Holy Spirit performed this work of prevention. There were prophets among them (Silas, for example) and it may be that a word of prophecy was given. It may have been by way of an inward impression upon their minds. It may have been outward circumstances. Only one thing is known to us — the only way to go was north-west.

Not only is there this negative, preventing work of the Spirit in guidance, there is also a positive aspect. He calls, sends and commissions. The vision of the man of Macedonia was just as much of the Spirit as was the preventing of the apostles from accomplishing their intended course.

Adoniram Judson, the apostle to Burma, knew this kind of guidance, preventing him from staying in India as he intended, driving him on instead to Burma and to greater usefulness. He and his wife Ann had been made *personae non gratae* in India and had been forced to sail from Calcutta to Madras, in southern India. John Waters relates the story: 'The Indian authorities had sent a message to Mauritius to tell the governor to keep watch on the missionaries. When they reached Madras on 4 June 1813, Adoniram and Ann saw that they were not going to be treated any better than before. As soon as the police found out that they had come, they sent off a report to the supreme government...There was no doubt that the Judsons would be deported to England as soon as the order reached Madras.

'There was no time to lose. Adoniram searched day and night for a ship. He hoped for one bound for the island of Penang, off the Malayan peninsular...but everyone he met in Madras seemed set on discouraging him from going anywhere near Burma. Missionaries would be persecuted, probably murdered. For a man life would be difficult, for a woman, impossible... At last, Adoniram found one. It was a dilapidated old boat, but it was the only one in the whole port ready to sail. He asked for its destination. The reply was completely unexpected. For a moment, Adoniram could not believe what his ears told him. The ship was bound for Rangoon — in Burma.'[1]

Clearly, the Holy Spirit drove the Judsons to Burma! We can now learn several lessons about guidance.

First, *God guides his children*. There are times when it is the most comforting thing of all to learn that God guides us. There have been times when we desperately needed to know his will. It is the wonderful lesson of Psalms 25 and 32 that God guides us. 'Show me your ways, O Lord; teach me your paths.

Lead me in your truth and teach me, for you are the God of my salvation; on you I wait all the day... The humble he guides in justice, and the humble he teaches his way' (Ps. 25:4,5,9). 'I will instruct you and teach you in the way you should go; I will guide you with my eye' (Ps. 32:8). God sends us the Holy Spirit as Christ's representative agent in our hearts with the stated aim of guiding us (Rom. 8:14). This is saying no more than that God takes a personal interest in our lives. We shall see in the next chapter how this truth comforted Joseph. It also proved a great help to Ruth.

No book (apart from Job) begins with such a picture of tragedy as that of Ruth. Within the space of a few verses we are introduced to her family only to find that the three leading male characters all die. Naomi, Ruth's mother-in-law, finds the experience of widowhood away from home in Moab so terrible that she calls herself Mara (meaning 'bitter'). Later Naomi can look back with some satisfaction that Ruth has found refuge 'under God's wings' and a godly, caring husband. Not only that, but Obed, her future son, became the father of Jesse, the father of David (Ruth 4:22). In the story of Naomi's life is the coming of Jesus (see the names of Boaz and Ruth in the earthly genealogy of Christ in Matthew 1:5)! Little wonder God was concerned to guide Ruth! The same God is at work in our lives.

Second, *we are all called to evangelistic activity.* There are, of course, special factors at work in this incident. Paul was an apostle and God called him by means of a vision (or possibly a dream). But the general truth is applicable to every Christian, for as we have already mentioned in the first chapter, every member of God's kingdom has a work of evangelism to do. We are all to hold fast our profession (Heb. 4:14), to hold fast the word of life (Phil. 2:16), to give a reason for the hope that is in us (1 Peter 3:15). A special blessing attends those who are instrumental in the conversion of others (James 5:20). Nor can anyone claim that due to personal factors they cannot possibly be expected to evangelize. Think

of Richard Baxter who, in the seventeenth century, was
instrumental in the conversion of almost the entire town of
Kidderminster. Amongst other ailments, he suffered from
incessant dyspepsia, kidney stones, headaches, toothaches,
swollen limbs, intermittent bleeding from various parts of his
body — and all this before the advent of modern pain-relieving
drugs.

From time to time we shall need encouragement in this
work. Paul received it in the form of another night-vision when
he came to Corinth. Having been persecuted at Philippi,
Thessalonica and Athens he was in need of being strength-
ened: when he arrived he preached with great fear and trem-
bling (1 Cor. 2:3). God came and spoke to his servant a word
that would greatly help him in the task ahead: 'Do not be
afraid, but speak, and do not keep silent; for I am with you, and
no one will attack you to hurt you; for I have many people in
this city' (Acts 18:9-10).

Pursuing a pathway of 'p's, God made a *promise* of his
presence and *protection* because he had a *purpose* to fulfil: the
salvation of many sinners in Corinth for which he would need
God's *power*. When we think of those who were converted,
Titius Justus (a distinguished Gentile), Crispus and Sosthenes
(leaders in the synagogue), Erastus (the city treasurer), Quar-
tus (a Roman citizen), not to mention the drunkards, homo-
sexuals, thieves and extortioners (1 Cor. 6:9-11), we can see
just how much Paul was in need of this promise.

Third, *guidance has negative and positive aspects to it*.
The Holy Spirit hinders and helps. In Acts 16 he closes and
opens 'doors' of opportunity. We have all known it so in our
lives. It is a matter of trusting his sovereignty and his wisdom.
All kinds of things happen to us that are totally beyond our
control. We can do nothing about them. It is the part of wisdom
to say that God is in charge of them all. Providence is his story!
'In all your ways acknowledge him and he will direct your
paths' (Prov. 3:6).

Not only is God sovereign, he is also wise. He knows what

he is doing. He always does everything in the right way and at
the right time. There are never any mistakes with God.
However difficult and frustrating the circumstances may be,
and we can only imagine the apostles to have arrived in Troas
in a state of confusion, God is at work. He never sleeps or
abdicates his power. Take the example of Paul's first impris-
onment in Rome. He writes to the Philippians who are discouraged by it all. The leading light of the gospel is under house-
arrest. The future of the church looks grim. The cause seems
lost. It is a time of worry and fear. But this is to distrust the
wisdom of God. So Paul reproves them, saying that it is not
like that at all: 'But I want you to know, brethren, that the
things which happened to me have actually turned out for the
furtherance of the gospel, so that it has become evident to the
whole palace guard, and to all the rest, that my chains are in
Christ; and most of the brethren in the Lord, having become
confident by my chains, are much more bold to speak the word
without fear' (Phil. 1:12-14).

Who says that when we are in trouble God isn't looking
after us? God's will may involve suffering (as it did in Joseph's
life) but in the overall scheme of things he is in complete
control.

Fourth, *guidance means using our intelligence!* This may
seem a surprising lesson from such a passage. After all, Paul
saw a vision! What Paul did after seeing this vision is of great
interest. 'Now after he had seen the vision, immediately we
sought to go to Macedonia, *concluding* that the Lord had
called us to preach the gospel to them' (Acts 16:10). Luke
(who has obviously now joined them, by his use of 'we') uses
a word which suggests that the apostles met together to
examine the evidence. They reasoned about it, asking all kinds
of questions as to the propriety of going over to Macedonia.
They did not simply take the vision as a sign without first using
their minds to examine the evidence.

If we want God to guide us we shall do the same thing. We
will need to *think*. 'Therefore do not be unwise, but understand

what the will of the Lord is' (Eph. 5:17). 'Do not be like the horse or like the mule, which have no understanding, which must be harnessed with bit and bridle, else they will not come near you' (Ps. 32:9). 'I beseech you therefore, brethren, by the mercies of God, that you present your bodies a living sacrifice, holy, acceptable to God, which is your reasonable service. And do not be conformed to this world, but be transformed by the renewing of your mind, that you may prove what is that good and acceptable and perfect will of God' (Rom. 12:1-2).

It is a false piety that demands inward impressions with no rational base, and declines to heed the constant biblical summons to use our minds and think it out in his presence. Five times in Psalm 119 (a psalm of wisdom) David calls out, 'Give me understanding' (vv. 34,73,125,144,169). Wise servants will do likewise.

Fifth, *guidance is not just a personal matter*. It is corporate. God guides through the counsel of friends and godly companions. We have already seen how important friends were to the apostle. He had with him Timothy, Silas and Luke. He consulted with them about this vision. He was prepared to take their advice and come to a collective decision.

We too shall need, as did Paul, to take advice from time to time. It is a sign of conceit and arrogance (not to say immaturity) to think that we always know best. In major matters of some importance to take advice is the best course of action. There are always people who know the Bible better than we do. A wise man takes advice (Prov. 12:15). 'Plans fail for lack of counsel, but with many advisers they succeed' (Prov. 15:22 NIV).

God guides by making known to us his wisdom. This he does through the church (Eph. 3:10). Labourers in the gospel have to take seriously the advice of the church as to their potential usefulness. Far too often folk felt called to ministry have ignored this advice, seeking admission elsewhere when an evangelical, and scripturally-based church says what they do not want to hear.

Learning these lessons will ensure that we walk in harmony with the Lord, who is at the same time 'the Lord Protector' who watches over us every step of the way. One day he will guide us home to be with himself for ever. Until then we cry:

Tis Jesus, the first and the last,
Whose Spirit shall guide us safe home;
We'll praise him for all that is past,
And trust him for all that's to come.

(Joseph Hart)

To see just how useful this truth can be in the lives of those who suffer we shall now take a look at Joseph.

3.
Man proposes, God disposes

God makes no mistakes. Knowing this can transform our lives! We have seen how necessary it is for us to *know* what God expects of us. We also need to be assured that, no matter what, God is in control of every event. When the going gets tough, this truth alone will keep us persevering.

Few people have been as useful as Joseph, and in days of difficulty he needed to be assured that God had not forsaken him. Joseph became second-in-command to the Egyptian Pharaoh (Gen. 41:40) at a time when Egypt had plenty of food, and famine threatened the existence of God's children in Canaan. That is a wonderful example of usefulness! But the journey to political fame and influence in Egypt was a difficult one which tested Joseph's commitment to follow the Lord at all costs. Psalm 105:19 summarizes it by saying, 'The word of the Lord tested him.' Jacob's favourite and pampered son found himself betrayed by his brothers, sold into slavery, traduced by an Egyptian general's wife and falsely imprisoned. Had God lost control? Where was God's guidance in all of this?

Guidance is always easier to see looking backwards — a bit like reading Hebrew, the Puritan Flavel once said. Joseph was able to say much later, 'And God sent me before you to preserve a posterity for you in the earth, and to save your lives by a great deliverance. So it was not you who sent me here, but God' (Gen. 45:7-8). Service for God is often prefaced by a time of learning in the harsh, and sometimes bitter, context of life's realities. Though Joseph was a dreamer (Gen. 37:1-11) he had first to shake off the timidity and arrogance of youth and learn that God uses those who are faithful to him, even when the going is tough.

Joseph had first of all to come to terms with the truth that his life, as every other, was in God's hands to do with as he willed. The forging of our wills to accept the truth that all things work together for our good (Rom. 8:28) is best learned on the anvil of experience. Joseph's summary statement of it in Genesis 50:20, 'God meant it for good...', was the result of years of firsthand experience whereby he had proved over and over again God's hand shaping every event in his life. What Joseph came to appreciate was the truth that there are no accidents in God's handling of our lives. It is only as we appreciate this that we can become useful for God. Failing to do so will commit us to a life of frustration and uselessness.

For me, learning this truth was difficult. It was the year 1978. I had just spent seven years studying: three in applied mathematics and another four at theological seminary. I was twenty-five, and ready for service. Or so I thought! All my wisest friends urged me in the direction of the preaching ministry, and my own inclinations were favourable to the idea. I felt I had a call to the ministry. Yet, no call was forthcoming! There were complications, of course. Not least was the fact that I had become a paedobaptist midway through my seminary training! This added to the difficulty of finding a suitable church. 'Why does God lead me all this way, only to find a closed door at the end?' I asked myself. For a whole year that door remained firmly closed. Interpreting providence at the time was both difficult and frustrating. Now, however, I can appreciate God's hand in it all. There were things I needed to learn — things which could not be learnt in any other way but in humble dependence on him.

Many of God's people have known times of frustration when life makes little sense. Sickness, bereavement, tensions in marriage, unemployment — these come into our lives like hammer blows. They often cause distrust and resentment to grow. They invariably slow us down, robbing us of days of usefulness when we felt close to God. Joseph was tested in precisely this way.

All of us are familiar with the words of Fanny Crosby's hymn:

> All the way my Saviour leads me:
> What have I to ask beside?
> Can I doubt his tender mercy,
> Who through life has been my guide?
> Heavenly peace, divinest comfort,
> Here by faith in him to dwell!
> For I know whate'er befall me,
> Jesus doeth all things well.

Joseph was a man who could echo just such a sentiment as this. In fact, he did so on several occasions during his fascinating life (Gen. 45:8; 50:20).

Joseph's brothers had sold him into slavery in Egypt and hoodwinked their father, Jacob, into believing that his son had been killed by some marauding wild beast. In Egypt Joseph, having landed himself into Potiphar's comfortable home (the captain of Pharaoh's guard), finds himself traduced by this man's wife, a venomous and affection-starved woman. He is falsely accused, summarily imprisoned without trial and without access to a lawyer! Later, God provides an opportunity for Joseph to use the one gift he has, interpreting dreams, which brings him into favour with Pharaoh — though only after a disappointing lapse of memory by Pharaoh's butler which only further tested poor Joseph's faith (Gen. 40-41).

Joseph had concealed his identity from his brothers, even to the extent of appearing to trick them by falsely accusing them of stealing and coming to Egypt under false pretences. The elaborate ritual in Genesis 44 whereby his brothers find the silver in their sacks of grain, and especially when Benjamin is found to have the Pharaoh's favourite drinking goblet in his sack, is all intended to bring them to see their own sinfulness. What is happening to them is precisely what had happened to Joseph by way of their former treachery. He had to teach them this lesson else they would not have been repentant.

Now, however, it was time for explanations. Would Joseph seek revenge? Would he throw them into prison? Would bitterness and seething resentment fuelled by years of frustration and anger now suddenly boil over when he faced his betrayers? How does one respond to such a series of calamitous events? One can grow bitter, cynical, angry, frustrated, or a combination of all four. It is one of Satan's devices to make us draw the conclusion that God has no use for us if we are in difficulties. The Puritan Thomas Brooks imagines Satan saying to a Christian in trial: 'Saith Satan, "Dost thou not see how Providence crosses thy prayers, and crosses thy desires, thy tears, thy hopes, thy endeavours? Surely if his love were towards thee, if his soul did delight and take pleasure in thee, he would not deal thus with thee."'[1]

Joseph's response is altogether different. He sees the providence of God in every detail of his life. That is the response of faith! 'But now, do not therefore be grieved or angry with yourselves because you sold me here; for God sent me before you to preserve life. For these two years the famine has been in the land, there are still five years in which there will be neither ploughing nor harvesting. And God sent me before you to preserve a posterity for you in the earth, and to save your lives by a great deliverance. So now it was not you who sent me here, but God', Joseph says to his brothers, 'and he has made me a father to Pharaoh, and lord of all his house, and a ruler throughout all the land of Egypt' (Gen. 45:5-8).

Now the tables are turned. And Joseph is magnanimous with them.

Far more significant than Joseph's personal magnanimity is the explanation he gives for the last twenty years in Egypt. It is, in fact, a confession of God's providence and care in the life of his servant.

God is in control

'It was not you who sent me here, but God,' Joseph says to his brothers (Gen. 45:8). Certainly his brothers had played a part. It was they who had felt the jealousy of their father's favour-itism towards their brother. It was they who saw him coming to Dothan and plotted to have him killed by abandoning him in a pit. It was they who experienced a change of heart and decided instead to make some financial gain by selling him as a slave to some passing Midianites. It was they, too, who had spun a plausible enough explanation to Jacob that wild beasts had killed him whilst they lovingly, but hypocritically, clutched a blood-stained coat, the symbol of all that Joseph meant to his grief-stricken father. They were culpable all right. But Joseph sees another's hand. 'God has been in control,' he says.

Four things seem to stand out.

First, *God is always watching over our lives*. He rules over every event. From the failure of the harvest, through the drought that had struck the land, to the disease that had blighted the crops — all of this was of the Lord. At one level the explanation is scientific: meteorological, biological and horticultural. At another level altogether it is the Lord's con-trolling hand. What had begun with a seemingly trivial request of Jacob's to send his son to Shechem to see how his other sons were getting along (Gen. 37:12-14) ended with enormous consequences that would bring the Lord's children into Egypt and keep them there for hundreds of years. This was God's great design all along!

Sinclair Ferguson has said, 'There are two ways of looking at life. It can be viewed simply in terms of what occurs.
That is what we popularly call "history". Christians, however,
can never be interested in human life merely to discover the
"when" or the "who" or the "what". They are always concerned to know the answer to the question "why" in order to
relate their answer to the biblical teaching of the purposes of
God.' [2]

Second, *God overrules the sinful actions of men.* When
Jacob died and his sons feared that this might provide Joseph
with an opportunity for revenge, Joseph reassured them with
these words: 'You meant evil against me, but God meant it for
good, in order to bring it about as it is this day, to save many
people alive' (Gen. 50:20). Men do things which are evil and
for which they are culpable, but God never abdicates his
control.

Peter explains Jesus' death this way: 'Men of Israel, hear
these words: Jesus of Nazareth, a man attested by God to you
by miracles, wonders, and signs which God did through him
in your midst, as you yourselves also know — him, being
delivered by the determined counsel and foreknowledge of
God, you have taken by lawless hands, have crucified, and put
to death; whom God raised up, having loosed the pains of
death, because it was not possible that he should be held by it'
(Acts 2:22-24).

There you have it: the most wicked action ever accomplished by men — the death of Jesus Christ! All kinds of
people were to blame for it: Judas, for he had betrayed Jesus;
the Jews, for by their complicity Barabbas had been released
instead of Jesus; Annas and Caiaphas, together with the entire
Sanhedrin court, for by their artifice they had tried Jesus and
found him guilty of blasphemy and treason; and Pilate, for by
his weakness he had allowed Jesus to be crucified. Yet it was
by God's set purpose and foreknowledge.

Third, *God overrules the free actions of men.* What

Joseph's brothers did, what the Jews did at Jerusalem was entirely unforced. Their decisions were uncompelled. There is no suggestion that God superintends in such a way that men are robots. Our thoughts are free — free, that is, within the limitations of our own sinful nature.

Scripture explains how King Ahab died this way. It is a most fascinating passage of Scripture (1 Kings 22:29-40). Ahab's life was doomed because of his insatiable wickedness: 'But there was no one like Ahab who sold himself to do wickedness in the sight of the Lord' (1 Kings 21:25). Elijah had delivered God's prophetic word: 'In the place where dogs licked the blood of Naboth, dogs shall lick your blood, even yours!' (21:19). But when the prophecy comes to be fulfilled it is put in this way. Ahab had disguised himself on the field of battle as an ordinary soldier and whilst in his chariot in the midst of the chaos of a battlefield 'a certain man drew a bow at random, and struck the king of Israel between the joints of his armour' (22:34). It was quite free and unsolicited, yet it fulfilled a prophecy of God. So are our thoughts and actions. 'The lot is cast into the lap, but its every decision is from the Lord' (Prov.16:33).

Fourth, *God overrules potentially hardening actions of men*. All of what happened to Joseph was potentially hardening. Joseph could have ended up a twisted, psychologically disturbed individual. There is some evidence to the effect that his father responded in just that way. Several times the darkness and bitterness of his soul reveal themselves. When after meeting Joseph, whom he had mourned as dead for twenty years, Pharaoh asks him how old he is (kings are allowed to ask such questions!), Jacob's reply is this: 'The days of the years of my pilgrimage are one hundred and thirty years; few and evil have been the days of the years of my life, and they have not attained to the days of the years of the life of my fathers in the days of their pilgrimage' (Gen. 47:9).

Poor old Jacob! Where is the joy at seeing Joseph again?

Only the dark side is to the fore. There is an expression in Welsh which I am told is a mark of the Celtic temperament: 'Y Ci Du'. It means 'the black dog' which is said to sit on your shoulder snarling and growling.

Joseph's response is again different. There is no hint of bitterness, but only sweetness and meekness. It is interesting to note that of the two who died on either side of our Lord, one responded with hardness and bitterness, hurling insults at him and saying: 'Save yourself and us', whilst the other responded with meekness and genuine repentance: 'And we indeed justly, for we receive the due reward of our deeds... Lord, remember me when you come into your kingdom' (Luke 23:39-42).

To summarize: God is always watching over us, making sure that everything is for our good. Nothing is beyond his ultimate control; his authority is beyond question even when we sin. How wonderful when we can learn this truth and respond like Joseph!

All four lessons are taught in a powerful and precise way in the *Westminster Confession of Faith* (chapter 5).

God rules. 'God the great Creator of all things doth uphold, direct, dispose, and govern all creatures, actions, and things, from the greatest even to the least, by his most wise and holy providence, according to his infallible fore-knowledge, and the free and immutable counsel of his own will, to the praise of the glory of his wisdom, power, justice, goodness, and mercy.'

God overrules sinful actions. 'The almighty power, unsearchable wisdom and infinite goodness of God so far manifest themselves in his providence, that it extendeth itself even to the first fall, and all other sins of angels and men; and that not by a bare permission, but such as hath joined with it a most wise and powerful bounding, and otherwise ordering, and governing of them, in a manifold dispensation, to his own holy ends; yet so as the sinfulness thereof proceedeth only from the creature, and not from God, who, being most holy and righteous, neither is nor can be the author or approver of sin.'

God overrules the free actions of men. 'Although in relation to the foreknowledge and decree of God, the first cause, all things come to pass immutably, and infallibly; yet, by the same providence, he ordereth them to fall out, according to the nature of second causes, either necessarily, freely, or contingently.'

God overrules potentially hardening actions of men. 'The most wise, righteous and gracious God doth oftentimes leave, for a season, his own children to manifold temptations, and the corruption of their own hearts, to chastise them for their former sins, or to discover unto them the hidden strength of corruption and deceitfulness of their hearts, that they may be humbled; and, to raise them to a more close and constant dependence for their support upon himself, and to make them more watchful against all future occasions of sin, and for sundry other just and holy ends.'[3]

Despite all that has happened to him, Joseph is still able to say, 'God has led me this way.' He has been guided by the Lord's own good hand. It is a promise that God makes to all his children: 'I will instruct you and teach you in the way you should go; I will guide you with my eye' (Ps. 32:8). 'The Lord will guide you continually, and satisfy your soul in drought, and strengthen your bones; you shall be like a watered garden, and like a spring of water, whose waters do not fail' (Isa. 58:11). It is the theme of Psalm 25: 'Show me your ways, O Lord; teach me your paths. Lead me in your truth and teach me, for you are the God of my salvation; on you I wait all the day,' David cries (vv. 4-5). And later in the psalm he is reassured by the promise 'Good and upright is the Lord; therefore he teaches sinners in the way. The humble he guides in justice, and the humble he teaches his way' (vv. 8-9).

God fulfils his plan and purpose

'And God sent me before you to preserve a posterity for you in the earth and to save your lives by a great deliverance,' Joseph says (Gen. 45:7). God had a plan and purpose in it all. That is always the way with providence. It is a matter of God working in history so as to conform everything to the 'counsel of his will' (Eph. 1:11). In the lives of all his children God fulfils his 'eternal purpose' (Eph. 3:11). God had a purpose in calling Abram from Ur of the Chaldees, when Isaac his son was given twin sons, Jacob and Esau, when Jacob finally married Rachel and two sons Joseph and Benjamin were born to them, when Jacob sent his son Joseph to check on his other children in Dothan, and when Joseph was betrayed and taken captive into Egypt.

There are times when we desire to be useful for God, but providence denies us the opportunity. At such times we shall have to be content to know that God is in control. His timing is perfect. He makes no mistakes. We need to trust him more than we do!

4.
Being different

D.L.Moody once said, 'A holy life will produce the deepest impression. Lighthouses blow no horns; they only shine.' Christian workers need to shine for Jesus Christ. Holiness in Christian service is essential.

The basic idea lying behind the adjective 'holy' is to be 'set apart', or 'different'. When Isaiah saw a vision of the holiness of God, he saw the Lord on his throne, and angels hovering all around calling one to another, 'Holy, holy, holy, is the Lord of hosts; the whole earth is full of his glory' (Isa. 6:3). Isaiah had seen Jesus in his glory (John 12:41).

God is so utterly different from us. By comparison Isaiah felt unclean and wretched. He felt there was no hope for him. There was, of course, as the passage later makes clear; the same God who is utterly holy is also the God who finds a way to forgive Isaiah's sin. God's holiness displays him as different from us. He is, as one theologian has expressed it, *'wholly other'*.[1]

The English language has no verb for 'holy' and instead we use the word 'to sanctify'. We often make the mistake of thinking of sanctification solely as the progressive work of putting to death remaining sin and becoming more like Christ. It does indeed mean this, but essentially a Christian is sanctified the moment he becomes a Christian. So, for example, when Paul writes to the Corinthians, he describes them as 'those who are sanctified in Christ Jesus, called to be saints' (1 Cor. 1:2). Believers *are sanctified!* Holiness is seen essentially as something God has already done in the life of a believer. Theologians often refer to this aspect of holiness as definitive (or relational, positional). Nor is this hard to understand: sin has been dethroned in his life, a new relationship exists with Jesus Christ, a new attitude has been developed towards the world. That is why believers are regularly called 'holy ones', or 'saints' (Acts 20:32; 26:18; 1 Cor. 1:2).

Our greatest need

Christians are meant to *be* different because they *are* different! God has made Christians different so that they might serve him. One of the ideas lying behind the use of the word 'holy' in the Bible is that of special usefulness. You see this in the Old Testament description of Aaron's garments (Exod.28:2). They were 'holy' in the sense that they marked him out as different from the rest. His clothes spoke of being special. The same can be said of the Sabbath (Gen.2:3), which is also described as holy ('sanctified'). This day is set apart and used in a different way from the other six days of the week. Then again, a part of the tabernacle is described as 'a Holy Place' (Lev. 16:2). Being curtained off from the rest of the structure, it was a special place with a special significance all of its own. Christians are 'a holy nation' (cf. 1 Peter 2:9). They have a special relationship to God that makes them different. As such they have a usefulness that is special too! Perhaps now we can understand why Robert Murray M'Cheyne once said that 'Our greatest need is our personal holiness.'

To see just how God underlined this truth in the minds of his people we turn to the example of Israel during the time of the prophet Samuel.

Israel was set apart as a holy nation. The Lord had a special usefulness for them to perform. But Israel did not like living in a theocracy. Somehow to be ruled directly by God was more than a little embarrassing for them. All around were the nations of the day, each one with their own king. But Israel had no king. And they wanted one.

Instead, they had Samuel. He was not a king, though his power and influence were enormous. He was first and foremost an Old Testament preacher. Technically he was the last of Israel's judges. And he was a great man of God. He had been given in answer to Hannah's prayer, raised by a godly priest called Eli and called into the ministry of God's Word whilst still relatively young. Samuel's usefulness is summed up in a brief statement: 'And the word of Samuel came to all Israel' (1 Sam. 4:1).

Now stick closely with me while we recall just what happened over a period of some twenty years (roughly, just over 1000 years B.C. and covering the five chapters 1 Samuel 4-8).

Quite early on in his life Samuel had witnessed the Ark of God being taken by the Philistines. It was a terrible day. The Philistines slew some 4,000 Israelites at Aphek and in a moment of unbridled haste and superstition the men of Israel thought that if only they carried the Ark into battle with them things would turn their way. It was to be a costly mistake. God honours those who repent and turn from sin, not those who perform acts of superstition. 30,000 men died in the battle, including Eli's two sons Hophni and Phineas. And when a Benjamite came running to tell poor old Eli the news, he fell over backwards in his chair and broke his neck. And Phineas' wife, pregnant at the time, went into premature labour surviving only long enough to see the child born and gasping his name, Ichabod: *the glory has departed.*

Slow learners

God was angry with his people for they had grown indifferent
to him. And this appears even more poignantly when we recall
that after the Ark was returned (it became too hot for the
Philistines to handle) it remained in Kiriath Jearim for a period
of twenty years.

It sometimes takes the Lord's people a long time to learn
certain lessons, as was the case here. This was a time of great
usefulness for Samuel. Up and down the land he preached to
and prayed with God's people calling upon them to forsake
their idols and return to the Lord. The great day came and the
people gathered at Mizpah. It was intended as a religious
gathering, but the Philistines thought to take advantage of the
situation. God is all-powerful and by a thunderstorm that
drove panic into the Philistine warriors they fled, pursued by
the Israelites. It was a great victory for Israel and a demonstra-
tion of what living in a theocracy meant. God was their King.
He would take care of them if only they would trust him. In
celebration of this great day Samuel erected a monument made
of stones and called it Ebenezer, recalling that this stone of
help was a symbol of how the Lord had helped them.

It seems altogether astonishing and ungrateful that the
very next incident that we read of is Israel's desire for a king
(1 Sam. 8:5). There was nothing wrong with a monarchy as
such. God had said to Jacob that kings would come forth from
his body (Gen. 35:11). And Moses had warned Israel that if
ever they were to choose a king it must be the man of God's
choice (Deut. 17:14-20). But it seems clear from 1 Samuel 8
that Israel desired a king *because they wanted to be the same
as everyone else.* They did not want to be different. They did
not want to depend upon God for everything.

They had just come through a period of reformation.
Twenty years after the battle of Aphek (when the Ark was
taken by the Philistines, cf. 1 Sam. 4:1) they were to experience one of those wonderful events in the history of the church

when God comes down in power. What a sight it must have been at Mizpah when the Philistines were sent packing at the noise of a thunderstorm from on high! Be honest! Haven't you dreamt about such days as this, when Israel 'put away the Baals and the Ashtoreths, and served the Lord only'? (1 Sam. 7:4).

Circumstances change. Samuel grew old; the people grew tired of him and his preaching. These had been days of peace with the surrounding nations when trading and commerce had grown. The horizons of the people had been enlarged. And they stood out like a sore thumb! Since the days of Moses, the Israelites had viewed God as their King. The Song of the Sea ends with those stirring words, 'The Lord shall reign for ever and ever' (Exod.15:18). Imagine an Israelite businessman trying to explain to his trading companion in far-away Greece (or with their near neighbours, the Canaanites) that back home they had no king except God! This was too embarrassing.

After all God had done for them, they were now prepared to cast him away. They wanted to be like all the other nations and using Samuel's age and the profligacy of his sons as an excuse, they said to him, 'Now make for us a king to judge us like all the nations' (1 Sam. 8:5).

So much for the history lesson. But what does it all mean?

A special relationship with God

Israel was a privileged nation. God had chosen them: first Abraham and his family, then Israel as a nation (Deut. 7:7; Isa. 41:8-9). He had shown them their chief end: to love him and enjoy him in return. This he did by systematically disclosing to them his character, their need and the way of salvation. Think of the covenant with Abraham, God's promise of restored fellowship received by faith alone. Think of the covenant with Moses where God makes two things clear: those who walk in fellowship with God must strive to be obedient to him, at the same time knowing that the law cannot possibly save anyone. Think of someone rubbing salt into an open wound and you will get the point of what this period of history is all about (not a covenant of works as is often thought: Paul makes it very clear in Galatians 3:15-25 that the covenant made with Moses did not set aside the one made with Abraham 430 years earlier). Then think of the Levitical sacrifices and priestly system revealing by way of pictures the way of salvation by the propitiatory death of a substitute; not just pictures, but smells — a few minutes in the sacrificial area of the tabernacle would turn the strongest of stomachs. This is God's way of telling us just how revolting sin is.

Israel had all this and much more, but they took it all for granted. They lusted after independence. And it's no different in our own day. Christian usefulness comes from remembering that we are the Lord's people. We are no longer the slaves of sin (Rom. 6:17). We are to rely upon God, acknowledging his power in our lives. As Dr Martyn Lloyd-Jones has said, 'To realize this takes away from us that old sense of hopelessness which we have all known and felt because of the terrible power of sin… How does it work? It works in this way: I lose my sense of hopelessness because I can say to myself that not only am I no longer under the dominion of sin, but I am under the dominion of another power that nothing can frustrate. However weak I may be, it is the power of God that is working in me.'[2]

God wants us to say, 'I'll follow him even if it means being different from everyone else!' But this is not the spirit of the age in which we live today. We have just passed through some twenty years of evangelical rethinking as to what constitutes a Christian life-style. Christians are wanting to know how far they can go, not what they are to deny themselves for the sake of God's kingdom. On my desk at present are books covering such areas as courtship and entertainment. It has now become fashionable to place emphasis upon Christian liberty and thus free Christians from the restraints of a fundamentalist

Christianity which had more to do with man-made rules and shibboleths than anything that Scripture had to say. But the pendulum has swung too far. Now Christians know their rights and want to use them as much as they dare.

A.W.Tozer once wrote an essay (of just two pages!) with the arresting title, *The True Saint is Different*. He commented: 'Men are impressed with the message of the Church just as far and as long as she is different from themselves...Let us plant ourselves on the hill of Zion and invite the world to come over to us, but never under any circumstances will we go over to them. The cross is the symbol of Christianity, and the cross speaks of death and separation, never of compromise. No one ever compromised with a cross. The cross separated between the dead and the living. The timid and the fearful will cry "Extreme!" and they will be right. The cross is the essence of all that is extreme and final. The message of Christ is a call across a gulf from death to life, from sin to righteousness and from Satan to God.'[3]

Christianity today is averse to self-denial (cf. Matt. 16:24; Mark 8:34; Luke 9:23). And yet Jesus made it a necessary condition of discipleship. Christians don't want to be different and as such betray the same concern for ease and floppiness that marked out ancient Israel. Christians feel free to adopt a life-style that is virtually no different from that of the world. It involves no cross-bearing. Ask yourself what rights have you forfeited for the sake of the kingdom? What things have you said 'No!' to, not because they were unlawful, but because they were inexpedient? (cf. 1 Cor. 10:23).

A prophet spurned

Samuel must have been saddened that his life's work seemed to have borne so little lasting fruit. There is a marvellous little verse tucked away in this passage telling us what Christians should do when they are sad and burdened. Here it is: 'But the thing displeased Samuel when they said, "Give us a king to judge us". So Samuel prayed to the Lord' (1 Sam. 8:6). What a lesson that is for us!

> What a Friend we have in Jesus,
> All our sins and griefs to bear!
> What a privilege to carry
> Ev'ry thing to God in prayer!
> O what peace we often forfeit,
> O what needless pain we bear,
> All because we do not carry
> Ev'rything to God in prayer.
>
> (Joseph Scriven).

God came immediately. Sometimes he makes us wait and the answer is then even more welcome when it comes; but not this time. Immediately, God gently put his arms around Samuel and reassured him that it wasn't Samuel that the people were rejecting, but him.

What are the consequences of going down a road of rejecting God? Samuel makes it plain to Israel: 'This will be the behaviour of the king who will reign over you: He will take your sons and appoint them for his own chariots and to be his horsemen, and some will run before his chariots. He will appoint captains over his thousands and captains over his fifties, will set some to plough his ground and reap his harvest, and some to make his weapons of war and equipment for his chariots. He will take your daughters to be perfumers, cooks, and bakers. And he will take the best of your fields, your vineyards, and your olive groves, and give them to his servants. He will take a tenth of your grain and your vintage, and give it to his officers and servants. And he will take your menservants and your maidservants and your finest young men and your donkeys, and put them to his work. He will take a tenth of your sheep. And you will be his servants. And you will cry out in that day because of your king whom you have chosen for yourselves, and the Lord will not hear you in that day' (1 Sam. 8:11-18). It is a picture of bondage and slavery. The road that looks so broad leads to death (Matt. 7:13-14). Israel was warned of the consequences of living to please oneself!

The New Testament elaborates on this theme. In the letter to the Hebrews we are led to believe that something has happened in their lives to dull the zeal of their devotion and consecration to God. They have, like ships without anchors, 'drifted away' (2:1); like arriving late for a meeting some have 'come short' instead of pressing on with haste (4:1,11). They have become 'sluggish' (6:12) and cast away their confidence (10:35).

As for reasons for this state of affairs, the writer to the Hebrews gives the following: a failure to deal seriously with indwelling sin which 'so easily ensnares' (12:1; Paul gives a similar warning in Romans 8:13 when he insists upon the necessity of mortification of sin); a tendency to become weary half-way through the race (12:3-4); and a failure to accept hardship and trials as God's way of training us and preparing us for greater things (12:5-11).

Slippery surface

Once you start going down the road of independence from God it's desperately hard to stop! Samuel knew all about this in his own family. His two sons had been raised under the most evangelical of influences, but they steadfastly marched down this road of independence and perished.

What happens if a person stops persevering? A whole theology of backsliding has comforted and reassured a countless number that they need not worry. They are 'carnal Christians' who will be saved in the end, because 'once saved, always saved'. But this is not the emphasis of Scripture. There are two passages in the letter to the Hebrews that are designed to give us a good shaking!

'It is impossible for those who were once enlightened, and have tasted the heavenly gift, and have become partakers of the Holy Spirit, and have tasted the good word of God and the powers of the age to come, if they fall away, to renew them again to repentance, since they crucify again for themselves the Son of God, and put him to an open shame' (6:4-6).

'For if we sin wilfully after we have received the knowledge of the truth, there no longer remains a sacrifice for sins, but a certain fearful expectation of judgement, and fiery indignation which will devour the adversaries of God' (10:26-27). These passages are not talking about true believers falling from grace, but pretenders whose falling away only reveals their unregenerate hearts. They begin well, but like Paul's friend Demas they fall in love with the world and drift away (2 Tim. 4:10). Like Israel in Samuel's day the allurement of the world becomes too strong. They want to be just like everyone else. And in so doing they forsake God.

Israel received just what they asked for! They were granted a king. Just the sort of man they wanted: worldly, arrogant and bordering on megalomania. Saul did not begin like that of course. But that is how he turned out eventually.

Prayer is a dangerous thing if our hearts are not in fellowship with God. There is that terrible warning in Psalm 106 which reminds us that God sometimes gives us just what we are so persistently asking for, in order to teach us a lesson or two: 'And he gave them their request, but sent leanness into their soul' (Ps.106:15). 'Give us a king,' Israel demanded. And God granted it. Within a few months they would learn to rue the day they ever asked for one.

Every now and then in our Christian lives the road begins to feel narrow and constraining. All around us are professing Christians whose lives are carefree. Perhaps you feel tempted to cross over to this broad road. *It is not the road that leads to life.* 'If anyone desires to come after me, let him deny himself, and take up his cross daily, and follow me. For whoever desires to save his life will lose it, but whoever loses his life for my sake will save it. For what advantage is it to a man if he gains the whole world, and is himself destroyed or lost? For whoever is ashamed of me and my words, of him the Son of Man will be ashamed when he comes in his own glory and in his Father's, and of the holy angels' (Luke 9:23-26).

If you want to be useful then you must be different: *swim against the tide!*

5.
Coping with immaturity

Service for God requires a level of maturity. There are some aspects of Christian work which cannot be done effectively by those who are novices (cf. 1 Tim. 3:6). As we have seen in the previous chapter, God's servants are to be different from everyone else. They are to be holy. They are to grow more like their Master. God's servants must grow in grace if they are to become useful for him (2 Peter 3:18). This will require both patience and perseverance: patience, because every one of us wants to be more useful than we are now; and perseverance, because if we stick at it we shall, with the Lord's help, become stronger and better able to cope with God's taxing demands. Overcoming immaturity is the way to usefulness. This is where the example of Timothy is of help to us.

Timothy was Paul's faithful helper in the work of the ministry (1 Cor. 4:17). For fifteen years Timothy accompanied the ageing apostle on his missionary journeys. Having been converted during Paul's first visit to Lystra when the apostle was stoned and left for dead outside the city (see Acts 14:6-20), Timothy had evidently grown substantially in grace by the time of Paul's return visit some one and a half to two years later — so much so that Timothy was asked to accompany him on his journeys (Acts 16:1-3).

The usefulness of some Christians is immediately evident.

At the end of the apostle's life, in a festering prison cell somewhere in Rome, he writes his second letter to Timothy, who by this time has been given the oversight of the work in Ephesus. Paul is concerned to write many things to Timothy. A young man with heavy responsibilities has to be careful over many things.

Paul's final charge to Timothy is set down in four crisp exhortations:

'Guard the good deposit that was entrusted to you' (2 Tim.1:14, NIV).

'Endure hardship as a good soldier of Jesus Christ' (2:3). .

'Continue in the things which you have learned' (3:14).

'Preach the word!' (4:2).

Chief among Paul's concerns is Timothy's usefulness: 'Therefore if anyone cleanses himself ... he will be a vessel for honour, sanctified and useful for the Master, prepared for every good work' (2 Tim. 2:21).

Timothy was called to be useful for God! What this means is spelt out in detail. He was to guard, continue in and preach the apostolic gospel. Six images define it further:

— like a soldier who cannot get involved in politics so Timothy will have to deny himself many things for the sake of the gospel (2:3,4);

— like an athlete who must compete according to the rules if he is to be sure of retaining his medal so God's servants are to be faithful (2:5);

— as a farmer must work hard to be sure of his crops so must God's servants be diligent (2:6);

— as civil engineers on Roman roads make straight paths so must God's useful servants keep strictly to the narrow path of God's revealed way (2:14-19);

— as slaves must not quarrel or gossip neither must God's servants if they are to be useful (2:23-26);

— just as in a large house there are all kinds of utensils, some more useful than others, so it is in God's house (2:20-21).

Pots and pans

It is this last illustration that brings out the idea of usefulness most clearly. In any large house there are 'vessels of gold and silver'; there are also vessels of 'wood and clay'. Some are for noble uses and others for ignoble. Paul's point is that there are ignoble teachers who are trying their best to veer the church away from the truth (like Hymenaeus and Philetus, see 2:17). To be useful, 'prepared for every good work' (v. 21), Timothy must pursue a holy life. But how? Timothy must seek to avoid the sins of youth: 'Flee also youthful lusts,' Paul says to him (v. 22).

In shaping Timothy's life for usefulness the Lord felt it necessary to point out a few home truths about his personality. Home truths are never welcome — unless they are seen as God's way of helping us come to terms with our besetting sins and failures and our resolve to deal with them. Timothy had many encouraging factors to help him grow in faithfulness, including the example of a godly home (1:3,5; 3:15), and the example of Paul which he had witnessed at first hand (1:13; 3:10). Timothy was also sensitive (witness his tears when he had to leave the apostle, 1:4), full of faith (1:5) and gifted with an unusual amount of self-discipline (1:7). There were also areas which were less than helpful to him: he was young (1

Tim. 4:12; 2 Tim. 2:22), delicate (witness his frequent ailments, 1 Tim. 5:23) and shy almost to the point of timidity (2 Tim. 1:7-8; 2:3; 3:12; 4:5). For Timothy to prove faithful he must take special care over certain sins. But what were they? The apostle may have had several in mind.

First, there is *pleasure*. Pleasure, in itself, is not wrong. The sensation of being pleased is a gift of God. We were made for pleasure: it is wrong to deny it. God made us to enjoy certain things and it is only a warped perspective on God's world (like Manichaeism) that sees it any other way. God 'gives us richly all things to enjoy' (1 Tim. 6:17).

What makes pleasure wrong is the attitude that goes along with it. If we pursue pleasure as an end in itself, then it is wrong. If our lives are out of balance, if we spend all our time and energy for pleasure — again we have got it wrong. Eating can be pleasurable, but if pursued in a certain way it can be a form of self-indulgence. The preacher who commends enjoyment (Eccles. 8:15) also castigates pleasure-seeking as an end in itself: 'Whatever my eyes desired I did not keep from them. I did not withhold my heart from any pleasure…and indeed all was vanity and grasping for the wind. There was no profit under the sun' (Eccles. 2:10-11).

The young are curiously self-indulgent. Craving after pleasure is one of the sins of youth. Those who would be useful for God need to know it, and beware of it. In particular, the pressure for sexual experimentation today is greater than perhaps in any other age. The need for clear and practical rules for Christian courtship is paramount. God's servants must learn to shine, and be different here. They must be models of consecration. Joseph's example — fleeing when the temptation to compromise is suggested — is what holiness means (see Gen. 39:6-12). Handsome as Joseph obviously was (Gen. 39:6), and persistent as Potiphar's wife most certainly was (Gen. 39:10), Joseph learned that the way to usefulness in God's kingdom was by saying 'No' — loudly and emphatically!

Second, there is *ambition*. Calvin thinks that this was

particularly in Paul's mind, for 'Having been led … to censure Hymenaeus and Philetus, whose ambition and vain curiosity had led them away from the faith, he again exhorts Timothy to keep at a distance from so dangerous a plague.' [1]

There is a time in our lives when all the great decisions have been made: the choice of a career, whether or not to get married and have a family and so on. But the young have all these decisions ahead of them. They are often daunting decisions, but not for the ambitious.

Ambition is a passion of the young. It is desire for success — which in most folk's eyes means houses, cars, holidays and bank balances. These are not wrong in themselves, but too often they are eagerly sought after without reference to what promotes the glory of God. The great Puritan Thomas Brooks had little time for the ambitious: 'Ambition is a guilded misery, a secret poison, a hidden plague, the engineer of deceit, the mother of hypocrisy, the parent of envy, the origin of vices, the moth of holiness and blinder of hearts, turning medicines into maladies and remedies into diseases… High seats are never but uneasy and crowns are always stuffed with thorns.' [2]

Ambition affects some of God's workers! There is an example of it in James and John, two of Jesus' disciples. It comes just as Jesus was foretelling his sufferings. The disciples were warned of the events that would befall their Master in Jerusalem by a three-fold announcement of impending suffering and death (Mark 8:31-2; 9:31; 10:33). In the final announcement he explained his mission in greater detail than he had ever done before. Jesus' coming was to end in self-denial. He was to be mocked, spat upon, flogged and eventually executed (10:33-34).

It seems almost beyond belief that it was just at this point that James and John, conscious that Jesus was about to usher in the Messianic Age, should stake their claim to a place of honour in this kingdom! They even prefaced their request with one of those open-ended claims for favour. 'Teacher,' they said, 'we want you to do for us whatever we ask' (v. 35). Children often ask such things when they know the answer is likely to be 'No!' But James and John weren't children! 'Grant us that we may sit, one on your right hand and the other on your left, in your glory' they asked (v.37). What a question at such a time! It was the outflow of ambitious hearts. It deserved the rebuke it got by way of reply: 'You do not know what you ask. Can you drink the cup that I drink, and be baptized with the baptism that I am baptized with?' (v.38).

Ambition is difficult to destroy and James and John were not about to give in yet. 'We can,' they replied. It must have been with a heavy heart that Jesus assured his two ambitious servants that they would indeed have a place of honour — in suffering, but it was the Father's prerogative to bestow places of honour at the Messianic Banquet. Little wonder that when the other disciples got to hear of this exchange they were furious with them!

Greatness in the kingdom of God is measured by faithful service. It is measured in reverse: not by climbing high in the estimation of others, but by descending into self-denial.

Third, there is *arrogance*. Arrogance is born of insecurity and inexperience. Those whose gifts have yet to be tested and proved sometimes feel the need to assert themselves. It is, or so they think, the only way to be noticed. They have too high an opinion of themselves.

Young people are by definition inexperienced. That is why arrogance can sometimes betray them. Those who have discovered the Reformed faith, for example, can sometimes lack the grace that is meant to accompany it. In their zeal to teach others the same truths they can cause irreparable damage, conveying more about themselves than the truth of God's Word. That is why, amongst other things, Timothy is told that workers for God must be gentle (2 Tim. 2:24).

Arrogance is the reflection of the image of Satan in the hearts of fallen humanity. It is the belief that we are always right, that we deserve what we are after, that all must yield to the principle, 'I should be at the centre of everything.' Its motto is 'My will be done.' This colours everything it seeks to do for God.

Arrogance has no place in the hearts of Christian workers. It is utterly contrary to the spirit of Jesus, 'who, being in the form of God, did not consider it robbery to be equal with God, but made himself of no reputation...' (Phil. 2: 6-7). He drew a veil over his native glory and showed himself to be a servant. *And we are to be of the same mind!*

Jesus Christ demands self-denial (Matt.16:24; Mark 8:34; Luke 9:23). It will involve the daily habit of putting to death (mortifying) every sin that remains in our hearts. Paul's command at this point is clear enough: 'For if you live according to the flesh you will die; but if by the Spirit you put to death the deeds of the body, you will live' (Rom. 8:13).

No one has taught us better of the need to mortify sin than the Puritan John Owen. His motto was: 'Kill a sin, or a part of a sin every day.' Sixty pages on 'The Mortification of Sin'[3] are amongst the best things written in Christian literature. The effect of allowing sin to go unchecked is to cripple effectiveness in Christian service. Says Owen: 'An unmortified lust will drink up the spirit, and all the vigour of the soul, and weaken it for all duties.'[4] When David allowed sin to reign in his life, indulging himself in both adultery and complicity in murder, he lost all his spiritual strength (Ps. 51:8). It robbed him of joy (v.12), worship (v.15) and a sense of God's presence (v.11). He was thereby unfit for service.

Owen sees a resemblance between a Christian and a typical garden: both have a potential usefulness, but only as the weeds are diligently uprooted: 'Mortification prunes all the graces of God, and makes room for them in our hearts to grow. The life and vigour of our spiritual lives consists in the vigour and flourishing of the plants of grace in our hearts. Now, as you may see in a garden, let there be a precious herb planted, and let the ground be untilled, and weeds grow about it, perhaps it will live still, but a poor, withering, unuseful thing. You must look and search for it, and sometimes can scarce find it; and when you do, you can scarce know it, whether it be the plant you look for or no; and suppose it be, you can make no use of it at all. When, let another of the same kind set in the ground, naturally as barren and as bad as the other, but let it be well weeded, and everything that is noxious and hurtful removed from it — it flourishes and thrives; you may see it at first look into the garden, and have it for your use when you please. So it is with the graces of the Spirit that are planted in our hearts. That is true; they are still, they abide in a heart where there is some neglect of mortification; but they are ready to die (Rev. 3:2), they are withering and decaying. The heart is like the sluggard's field — so overgrown with weeds that you can scarce see the good corn. Such a man may search for faith, love, and zeal, and scarce be able to find any; and if he do discover that these graces are there yet alive and sincere, yet they are so weak, so clogged with lusts, that they are very little use; they remain, indeed, but are ready to die. But now let the heart be cleansed by mortification, the weeds of lust constantly and daily rooted up (as they spring daily, nature being their proper soil), let room be made for grace to thrive and flourish — how will every grace act its part, and be ready for every use and purpose!'[5]

The only way to deal with arrogance (as well as every other sin) is to constantly weaken it. This is what Owen has to say: 'As a man nailed to the cross; he first struggles, and strives, and cries out with great strength and might, but, as his blood and spirits waste, his strivings are faint and seldom, his cries low and hoarse, scarce to be heard; when a man first sets on a lust or distemper, to deal with it, it struggles with great violence to break loose; it cries with earnestness and impatience to be satisfied and relieved; but when by mortification the blood and spirits of it are let out, it moves seldom and faintly, cries sparingly, and is scarce heard in the heart; it may have sometimes a dying pang, that makes an appearance of great vigour and strength, but it is quickly over, especially if it be kept from considerable success.'[6]

Serious dealings with the sin that remains in our lives will open up new doors of usefulness. A failure to do so will cause these doors of opportunity to shut firmly in our face.

Ants and sluggards

Satan tempts the young with ambition and arrogance. He also lures them to beds of ease. It is expected of children that they find 'play-time' more rewarding than hard work! Growing up, however, means putting away childish things (1 Cor. 13:11). It means eating solids rather than milk (Heb. 5:12), graduating from school and moving on to university (Heb. 6:1). Those who would be useful for God must be prepared to work hard for him. They must be prepared to suffer for Christ.

This is what Timothy was urged to consider: 'You therefore must endure hardship as a good soldier of Jesus Christ' (2 Tim. 2:3). Just as the apostle had himself suffered, Timothy could not expect any different (2:9). It was something which Paul had learned when he first encountered Timothy in Lystra when he had been beaten senseless and left for dead outside the city: 'We must through many tribulations enter the kingdom of God' he recalled (Acts 14:22).

Many proverbs make the point clear. The lazy man finds it difficult to get up in the morning. He turns over and over — as though hinged to his bed (Prov. 26:14). He refuses to go outside, insisting that a lion is waiting for him! (22:13; 26:13). Ask this man, 'When are you going to rise from your bed?' and he has no answer: 'A little sleep, a little slumber, a little folding of the hands to sleep' (6:10). Like the little boy whose mother has to tell him twenty times to finish his dinner, he finds that half way through it has got too cold to eat (19:24; 26:15). If only we could learn from the lowly ant!

'Go to the ant, you sluggard!
Consider her ways and be wise,
Which, having no captain,
Overseer or ruler,
Provides her supplies in the summer,
And gathers her food in the harvest. '

(Prov. 6:6-8).

The reference here is to the harvester ant, commonly found in the desert. Colonies can consist of up to a million ants, the vast majority being sexless workers and soldiers. Unquestioning obedience and hard work — that is what an ant can teach us!

When we look through the pages of church history we find hundreds of examples of brave men and women who endured hardship for the sake of the kingdom of God. There is the saintly Bishop of Smyrna, Polycarp who, after serving Christ for eighty-six years, was finally killed for refusing to deny his Lord. 'How can I deny him who has never done me any harm?' he said. Or there is the zealous William Tyndale who defied the king and translated the Bible and was eventually burned to death in Belgium by the edict of Henry VIII.

One also thinks of Latimer and Ridley, two great English Reformers who were both burnt at the stake, a brother of Ridley placing gunpowder around their necks so as to hasten the end for them both. Latimer's came quickly, but Ridley's fire had been poorly made and he had to suffer the loss of both legs before the fire reached the gunpowder which finally killed him. In the midst of it all rang out words of faith and trust in the God of all grace.

We think also of the moving story of the Wigtown martyrs in 1685, Margaret Lachlison and Margaret Wilson. Having refused to take the 'oath of abjuration' (denying the Solemn League and Covenant) they were sentenced to be drowned in the Solway Firth. Margaret Lachlison was seventy and tied to a post just below the high water mark while her companion

Margaret Wilson, just eighteen years old, was tied closer to shore. It was hoped that having seen the old woman drown she would be spared the same fate by her recantation. When the older woman had drowned she was asked what she thought, to which she replied, 'What do I see but Christ wrestling there?' As the tide came in further she read from Romans 8, repeating the last few verses: 'Who shall separate us from the love of Christ?...in all these things we are more than conquerors through him that loved us.' Turning down a final opportunity to save herself she said, 'I will not. I am one of Christ's children; let me go.' And so she died, another of God's heroes, and useful to the end.

An easier way?

Today's Christianity is different. It is about success and glamour. A 'health and wealth' gospel promises a life of miraculous healing, unlimited prosperity and freedom from all kinds of taboos that restricted Christians in the past. It is a flabby, sickly Christianity.[7] Its motto of 'name it and claim it' (or as someone has put it, 'gab it — grab it') has a huge following. In its wake comes a host of moral and spiritual problems. It is far from the self-denying, cross-bearing insistence of Jesus. Whatever we think of parts of Bonhoeffer's theology we can but admire his stand as he wrote, 'When Christ calls a man he bids him come and die.' Eight years later he was hanged by the Nazis.

The final entry in Jim Elliot's *Journal* reads as follows:

Dec 31 (1955): A month of temptation. Satan and the flesh have been on me hard. How God holds my soul in His life and permits one with such wretchedness to continue in His service I cannot tell. Oh, it has been hard... I have been very low inside me struggling and casting myself hourly on Christ for help.

Marriage is divorce from the privacy a man loves, but there is some privacy nothing can share. It is the knowledge of a sinful heart.

Four days later he was speared to death by Auca Indians. For ten years after that, his wife Elisabeth Elliot (they had been married for barely two years) remained with the tribe that had killed her husband as a witness to the power of Christ in the lives of his people.[8]

Most Christians have times when they long to be useful. They want to be all-out for God. They want their lives to be lived in close and unbroken fellowship with God. They want to be like Samuel: 'Speak Lord, for your servant is listening' (1 Sam. 3:10 NIV); or Isaiah: 'Here am I, send me!' (Isa. 6:8 NIV). Is this how you feel as you read these pages? Then you must be like Timothy — faithful!

6.
Don't worry!

Stress can be a positive help to usefulness. Paul confesses to have been under stress during his time at Corinth (1 Cor. 2:3) and look at how useful that ministry proved! But if certain stresses are helpful, others are not.

Worry, in particular, cripples usefulness. Think of the Israelites exiled in Babylon and sitting under willow trees (Ps. 137), Elijah under a juniper tree (1 Kings 19), or Jonah under another tree of sorts (Jonah 4) and you will see what I mean. In each case energy and enthusiasm for God's work are sapped.

Amateur psychoanalysis can be a dangerous thing. Dr Gaius Davies cites the case of a warning given by an American psychologist to his students: 'Think of being attached as aptitude testers to an army base camp in the Sinai desert. A young man is brought in with a severe stammer, and he has a history of being a bit of a psychopath who covered up a killing which he performed in a temper. The details of his birth and upbringing are uncertain, with stories of being found in a river and being brought up at court. He also reports strange sights in the desert: a burning bush and a voice speaking to him. Would the staff psychologist have recognized Moses, or failed him in all the tests?'[1]

Clearly, we need to be careful in analysing others! Even

so, we all recognize that some people, some Christians, suffer from problems caused by the stresses of this life. They are the 'walking worried'. The next time you sing William Cowper's hymn:

> God moves in a mysterious way
> His wonders to perform;
> He plants his footsteps in the sea,
> And rides upon the storm

spare a thought for Cowper himself. For most of his life he suffered from clinical depression, often expressing his darkest thoughts in his poems.

Despite the friendship and counsel of his good friend, John Newton, Cowper knew recurring bouts of illness. One of his last poems reflected on the story of a castaway who had fallen overboard in mid-Atlantic. Sailors had tried to rescue him, but had failed. Cowper wrote,

> No voice divine the storm allay'd
> No light propitious shone;
> When, snatch'd from all effectual aid
> We perished each alone:
> But I beneath a rougher sea,
> And 'whelmed in deeper gulphs than he.[2]

Cowper, who in this poem believes himself to be in a worse condition than a drowning man at sea, was not alone in his sufferings. We have already mentioned Elijah, Jonah and the Israelites. To that we can add David(Ps. 42, 43), and Jeremiah (Jer. 20:14-18). In addition we may add the names of John Bunyan, Martin Luther and Charles Haddon Spurgeon, all of whom describe conditions of 'depression' at some time in their lives. A stark reality faces us: mature Christians can, and do, suffer from depression which often robs them of opportunities for usefulness.

It is, therefore, all the more surprising that Christians (in general) show little sympathy for the depressed. The usual response is to suggest that all such states are a result of repressed guilt due to unconfessed sin, or (worse still) that it is wrong for a Christian to be sad and unhappy (thereby adding to the problem of depression further feelings of guilt).

To see the effects of stress on usefulness we shall take a brief look at three Old Testament prophets: Elijah, Jonah and Jeremiah.

Food and water!

The causes of depression are complex, but some have fairly simple explanations. Elijah is a case in point. When the Lord finds Elijah near Beersheba sitting under the juniper tree (1 Kings 19:1-9) praying that he might die, the counsel he received was anything but spiritual (at least in the sense that we often take the word 'spiritual' to mean). Twice, God sends an angel who gently wakes him from his sleep and insists that he eats something. There were no lectures on the sin of depression. Elijah wasn't told that he should be H-A-P-P-Y all the day! Nor was he counselled to read his Bible and spend some time in prayer. Instead, Elijah is given food and water. Just as important, Elijah is allowed to go to sleep (1 Kings 19:6). And in this seemingly unspiritual episode there lies a great deal of profound advice to every Christian.

Elijah was tired. He had just fought the battle of his life against Ahab and his wicked men. On Mount Carmel Elijah had faced the most severe test of his faith. It was to be the moment of supreme usefulness of the prophet of God!

Every ounce of his being had been involved in the battle against Ahab. Imagine how tired he would be after slaughtering the bull for the sacrifice with his own bare hands (1 Kings 18:23). Adrenalin would be flowing through every artery and vein in his body as he challenged the prophets of Baal to demonstrate the reality of their god. Finally, with the welter of emotions (exhilaration, courage, fear, tension) draining his body (and mind!), having been up all night, he repaired the altar, dug a trench, cut the bull into pieces and urged the false prophets to fill the trench with water. Then followed a prayer (in the hearing of all his opponents) that God would come and reveal himself in their midst. Afterwards he would have to slaughter the false prophets.

Nor was this all. Earnest prayer (seven times) for rain followed, draining Elijah of every last ounce of his strength (1 Kings 18:42-45). Added to all of this was the fact that Ahab escaped to Jezreel where Jezebel (Elijah's most fierce enemy) lay ready to kill him given the opportunity.

It is at this point that Elijah (after an exhausting run to Jezreel ahead of Ahab) is overcome with depression. The battle was not over yet: indeed, the worst was yet to come. Already Elijah felt he could not carry on. Everything in him cried out 'Enough!' So he prayed that God should take away his life.

A man of like passions

Elijah is not alone in these feelings. Christians who have suffered long periods of illness, weakening not only the body but the very resolve to live, have known these thoughts. Indeed, two of the most useful servants I have known have tragically taken their own lives. Depression got the worse of them. It was a test they found unable to conquer.

To a lesser degree, 'workaholics' know these feelings every so often. Christians who find themselves breaking God's rules for adequate rest: ministers who never take a day off, busy Christians whose Sundays are busier than any other day, ambitious career- orientated men and women who sacrifice basic rules of health — not eating regular meals, not taking adequate time when they do eat, 'burning the candle at both ends' — these often find themselves overtaken by this 'Elijah complex', not a desire to die so much as a desire that things were different from what they are.

The lesson is clear: God sanctions the use of common sense when it comes to this kind of depression. Are we taking enough rest? Are we eating properly? Are we balanced in our attitude to work? Is our career getting in the way of our spiritual and physical/mental well-being?

In the church especially, we need to take good care of God's useful servants. Most churches have a few people who seem to do everything. They sit on every committee, they are present at every meeting, they are expected to do everything: 'A willing horse' so the saying goes 'is never idle.' It never occurs to some that a man's usefulness is seriously undermined when over-used. The church needs to cultivate a 'team ministry' (or 'body-life' as the current jargon has it), by which we mean that every member has a part to play. This, in case you have forgotten, is what this book is all about!

The fact that Elijah's depressive reaction to stress was largely physical in explanation also helps us to come to terms with modern physiological explanations of depression. It is now widely recognized that depression is caused by the lack of amines (substances which help form the neurotransmitters of the brain and nervous system). The careful and prescribed use, therefore, of anti-depressants (which stimulate the production of amines) is God's way of helping certain Christians through a period of stress. The fact that it is seen to be less 'spiritual' than a course of prayer and fasting ought not to be condemned any more than God's prescription of good food and sleep to Elijah.

The case of Jonah is quite different.

On the run?

Jonah was a servant of God (2 Kings 14:25). He had been

called to service in the kingdom of God (Jonah 1:1-2). And like Elijah, Jonah too was to witness God's power. Anyone spending three days and nights inside the stomach of a whale and emerging relatively unscathed has to have witnessed the power of God!

Like Elijah, Jonah was also tired: physically and emotionally drained following the stormy sea-voyage, the near drowning as he was hurled overboard, the traumatic incident with the whale, and especially the sense that after all he was running away from God!

Disobedience to God can cause severe problems in our emotional, psychological and spiritual well-being. Jonah was a disobedient prophet who could not square God's love for his avowed enemies — the Ninevites. He could not face the slight made to his reputation and pride if he were to go back telling of how he had preached forgiveness to their enemies. God had asked Jonah to sacrifice too much, or so he thought. And Jonah was angry.

Jonah had been on the run from God — or, to put it in another way, God was pursuing Jonah. No matter how far away Jonah ran (he took a journey in the exact opposite direction to Nineveh) he was confronted by the presence of God. Jonah demonstrates his anger on a vine which grows and provides shelter for a while and then withers and dies. He shows all the classic signs of depression: immobility, irritability, a refusal to see sense. Nor is Jonah's sense of frustration unique. How often has God called on us to do things we would rather not have to do? And in refusing to do them, how often have we also known the consequent guilt and frustration that ensues? We may not have expressed it quite as boldly as Jonah ('Better to die than to face the all-piercing eye of God'), but we all know only too well the symptoms of this problem.

Jonah's depression is the result of a theological error: he distorted the truth about the scope of God's grace. Wrong thoughts about God stubbornly held can lead to serious consequences. As Sinclair Ferguson has put it, 'Prejudices (that is, for the Christian, judgments and opinions which are formed without knowledge of the circumstances, and not from the standpoint of God's Word) can daily drive us from the love of our fellows and from the service of God to them.'[3]

Nor were his problems merely theological; Jonah was guilty of wilful disobedience. He insisted that he was right and showed every determination to carry through a course of action to prove it. The Lord challenged Jonah, reasoning with him by means of a vine which grew and then died, that Jonah had no right to be angry with it (since he hadn't caused it to grow in the first place). Similarly he had no right to refuse God's grace to the Ninevites. God will have mercy upon whom he will have mercy. Jonah must humble himself and obey the Lord!

Gently, but firmly, the Lord challenged Jonah's depression. It was the result of sinful behaviour patterns on Jonah's part. And sin (ultimately) can never go unchallenged. That is why we find David challenging himself: 'Why are you downcast, O my soul? Why so disturbed within me? Put your hope in God, for I will yet praise him, my Saviour and my God' (Ps. 42:11 NIV).

Coping with rejection

In addition to Elijah and Jonah, the Bible alludes to Jeremiah's depression.

Jeremiah's personality is the most well-defined in the Old Testament. Unlike some of the other prophets who reveal almost nothing of themselves, Jeremiah makes a series of graphic allusions to the way he felt. Called upon to deliver a message of repentance to a people who seemed beyond any sense of contrition, Jeremiah despairs of ever finding comfort:

'I would comfort myself in sorrow;
My heart is faint in me...
I am mourning;
Astonishment has taken hold of me.
Is there no balm in Gilead,
Is there no physician there?
Why then is there no recovery
For the health of the daughter of my people?'

(Jer. 8:18,21-22).

They hated his message, branded him a traitor, persecuted and finally imprisoned him. All his youthful dreams were shattered so that he despaired of life:

'Woe is me, my mother,
That you have borne me,
A man of strife and a man of contention to the whole earth!
I have neither lent for interest,
Nor have men lent to me for interest.
Every one of them curses me.'

(Jer. 15:10).

'Cursed be the day in which I was born!
Let the day not be blessed in which my mother bore me!
Let the man be cursed
Who brought news to my father, saying,
"A male child has been born to you!"
Making him very glad.
And let that man be like the cities
Which the Lord overthrew, and did not relent;
Let him hear the cry in the morning
And the shouting at noon,
Because he did not kill me from the womb,
That my mother might have been my grave,

And her womb always enlarged with me.
Why did I come forth from the womb to see labour and
    sorrow,
That my days should be consumed with shame?'

(Jer. 20:14-18).

Perhaps you haven't read these words for some time and find
them shocking. They are! The Bible pulls no punches when it
reflects on the spiritual struggles of some of its characters.
Perhaps you have never expressed your anxiety quite as
openly as Jeremiah, but you too have felt something of this
black despair crippling your usefulness.

What these three cases tell us is that Christians are not
exempt from depression. We need to be careful so as not to
suggest that they always fall into these three categories. The
causes may be immensely difficult to unravel. It may be due
to problems experienced early in childhood (e.g. separation
and/or divorce of one's parents), an inability to cope with the
pressures of adolescent life (e.g. courtship) or the stress of
modern urban living (e.g. handling the relationship between
'what I need' and 'what I want' in terms of money, home, life-
style). It may be the inability to cope with sudden bereavement, or the onset of old age. The causes can be physical (e.g.
hormonal, or what one wag calls 'blue genes'), or spiritual (the
loss of assurance, e.g. Isa. 50:10), and often the one affects the
other.

High standards

Nor should it be thought strange that Christians suffer from
symptoms of depression. They, after all, set themselves goals
which they never reach: they strive for perfection and never
attain it. The good they would do is always hampered by the
presence of evil indwelling their hearts. Every day brings a

fresh load of sin to confess and new battles to be fought (cf. Rom. 7:18-19; Gal. 5:17-18). Paul learned the lesson at the very start of a missionary career, that it is through many trials that we all enter the kingdom of God (Acts 14:22). Later, he underlined it by adding that he was harassed by 'conflicts on the outside, fears within' (2 Cor. 7:5 NIV). The mixture of guilt and failure is potentially explosive. Small wonder that many psychiatrists have blamed religion for most, if not all, problems of the mind.

Added to this is the presence of Satan — a roaring lion always on the lookout for prey (Eph. 6:12; 1 Peter 5:8). To be sure it is possible to fall into the trap of a morbid preoccupation with the devil (current views of demon possession and exorcism go way beyond what we find in the Bible itself!). C.S.Lewis, in the preface to *The Screwtape Letters*, wrote that 'There are two equal and opposite errors into which our race can fall about devils. One is to disbelieve in their existence. The other is to believe, and to feel an excessive and unhealthy interest in them.'[4]

Nevertheless, we are to be on guard against the devil's wiles and devices. William Gurnall's classic book *The Christian in Complete Armour* (written in a time when witches were being hunted and burned) is a masterpiece of sane and practical help to the Christian in combating the onslaughts of the devil.[5]

All three areas (the world, the flesh and the devil) pose for the Christian a potential point of crisis. In addition there are assemblies where the rule is authoritarian and legalistic, going beyond the Bible's norms, ignoring privacy and liberty of conscience. In such assemblies sensitive Christians can be made to feel failures and utterly useless.

What can be done?

First we need to recall that coping with stress is part of what life is all about. But, as we suggested at the very beginning of this chapter, not all stress and worry is wrong. Despite the frequent citation of texts such as: 'Therefore I say to you, do not worry about your life...' (Matt. 6:25) and 'Be anxious for nothing...' (Phil. 4:6), they are still often misunderstood. A certain amount of stress (worry, anxiety) is normal.

Feeling stress is a built-in device to signal danger. To avoid an oncoming car travelling at speed in the same lane as yourself it is the body's quickening heart rate, fast breathing (following a moment of holding one's breath), sweaty palms, a feeling of weakness in the knees etc. that alerts you to the danger. If an athlete never felt a degree of tension he could never win a race. For that matter, a preacher needs a certain amount of butterflies in his stomach if he is to preach well (cf. Paul at Corinth, 1 Cor. 2:3). Shakespeare caught the idea superbly when he has Henry V (rallying his troops at Agincourt) say, 'Imitate the action of a tiger; stiffen the sinews, summon up the blood.'

It is a most wonderful truth that Christ himself had moments of fear when his soul was overwhelmed by the possibilities that lay before him (cf. Mark 14:33). It is not stress as such that the Bible condemns, but excessive stress. And it is when anxiety goes beyond what is necessary to meet the situation that it becomes excessive.

Second, we need to be far more sympathetic to those who fail to cope with excessive stress. Anxiety can lead to all kinds of problems: phobias, obsession, hysteria, withdrawal or depression. As we have already seen the reasons for such breakdowns can be many. But whatever the reason the church needs to learn to show love and compassion to the depressed.

One of the great needs of our time is the ministry of encouragement. It is interesting that Barnabas was surnamed the son of encouragement, reflecting in his name the ministry of the Holy Spirit as a helper and encourager (Acts 4:36; cf.11:23). We need more like him, especially in encouraging run-down workers. Why are there Christians who feel unloved, unwanted and useless? Is it because we have ignored their usefulness, failed to encourage them, taken them for granted, given them too much to do?

In 1856, in the Surrey Gardens Music Hall there occurred a disaster, the effects of which were to haunt Spurgeon for the rest of his life. The auditorium was said to have seated 10,000 and just at the moment when Spurgeon began to pray, someone shouted 'Fire!' In the panic that ensued miraculously only seven people were killed (and twenty-eight injured), but the effects of it damaged Spurgeon psychologically. He often suffered from bouts of depression (made worse by the onset of gout and a case of small-pox). On at least one occasion he lost his nerve while preaching and frequently he made arrangements for others to take his place.[6]

What happened to Spurgeon can happen to any Christian. And the church needs to be a community of love and fellowship. Far too often the church is riddled with cliques and factions. Too often we are too engrossed in our own affairs, showing little concern for others. Too often the lack of discretion shown by Christians means a fear to open up one's heart to another. And too often Christians are heard to say, 'The last place I'd look for help is in the church!'

Third, the fact that there are an estimated seventeen million schizophrenics in the world (yes, seventeen million!) and that depression is one of the commonest reasons for visiting the doctor ought, at the very least, to say something to the church. We are complex beings whose minds and bodies intimately relate with one another. Just as we need a trained doctor to deal with physical illness, so we (sometimes) need skilled 'doctors of the mind' to deal with mental illness. Ministers ought to have certain skills in counselling. But however skilled a minister may be, there are certain conditions which need expert handling. The church must educate itself into the belief that it is not wrong to seek such help. The church needs useful counsellors too.

Useful books:
J. White: *The Masks of Melancholy. A Christian Psychiatrist Looks at Depression and Suicide* (IVP)
G. Davies: *Stress: The Challenge to Christian Caring* (Kingsway)
J. Edwards: *The Religious Affections* (Banner of Truth).

7.
Useful in reformation

As a boy, I recall being a fan of *Dr Who*. It was not the inane story line so much that grabbed my attention — though the very thought of those Daleks still causes me some unease. Rather, it was that time-machine. The very thought of being able to step into a 'police-box' (for that is what, externally at least, it was) and be taken to any period of time one cared to choose was (and still is) enormously appealing.

Several important dates come to mind. I would like to stand at the bottom of the steps of the Castle Church in Wittenberg and watch an Augustinian monk by the name of Martin Luther nail a piece of parchment to the great doors upon which he had written ninety-five theses in defiance of the major claims of the Roman Catholic Church.

If possible I should like to be taken back to almost any year from 1735-45 and witness the Great Awakening under such preachers as the Wesleys, George Whitefield, Daniel Rowland and Howel Harris in England and Wales, or the Tennents, Jonathan Edwards and David Brainerd in New England.

My greatest wish would be to walk down the streets of Geneva some time during the years 1540-50 and take a pew inside St Peter's Cathedral and listen to John Calvin give one of his daily expository sermons.

You note I avoid all the persecuting times! I avoid mentioning too, a desire to have seen our Saviour. I'm not sure of my motives when I say I would like to have sat on the hillside west of the Sea of Galilee and heard Jesus deliver the 'Sermon on the Mount', or to have been in Jerusalem during those turbulent last days before his execution.

One event I would like to have seen was a reformation! To see a reformation is to witness some of God's giants at work. We have been stressing in these pages the fact that all of us have a task to do. No Christian is meant to be idle. But a glimpse at a giant in terms of gifts and ability at this stage will bring what we have been thinking about into perspective, for here and there God gives some servants five talents, as opposed to just two or one (Matt. 25:14-30). Ezra was just such a 'five-talent' man.

Ezra appears as a reformer in one of the many reformations that took place during Old Testament times. There were several: at the end of Joshua's life (Josh. 24); during the reign of three great and godly kings, Asa (2 Chr. 15), Hezekiah (2 Chr. 29-31) and Josiah (2 Chr. 34-35). The one that we shall consider is during the lives of Ezra and Nehemiah.

Thank God for the Reformation

To think that a reformation is something that took place only once in the sixteenth century is a grave mistake. Whenever God has been pleased to root out superstition and error and vindicate his truth, restoring in the church a love for, and commitment to, the Bible as the only rule of faith and practice, then reformation has taken place. Even as I write, to my left is a picture of Luther on which are the words: 'Thank God for the Reformation. Pray for another one!'

After the Babylonian exile had come and gone, and the Persians had risen in power, some of God's people returned to

Jerusalem. There was an initial return under Zerubbabel and
Jeshua (to rebuild the temple). There followed, some sixty
years later, another return under Ezra (to finish the temple
which had come to a halt due to opposition from Samaritan
quarters), and again, some twenty years after that, a return
under Nehemiah (to build the walls of Jerusalem).

When everything had been completed, a feat which
needed the full support of all the people, a great celebration
was planned at which Ezra was asked to preach. The books of
the Law (what was then available of the Old Testament) had
been long since forgotten. Ezra emerges as a reformer in the
tradition of John Calvin or John Knox. He is a model of what
a preacher should be.

What, I wonder, do you look for in a minister? What are
your expectations as you come to church on Sunday morning?
It is a matter of fact that preaching is regarded as an out-moded
form of communication today. The most common usage of the
word 'preaching' is by way of disdain: to preach at someone
is to deliver moralistic pronouncements in a manner calculated to wound. Even amongst God's people there is a low
level of expectation as to preaching.

When Peter, for example, suggests that a preacher speaks
'the oracles of God' (1 Peter 4:11), or when Paul throws in the
off-hand remark that an unbeliever who hears a prophecy in
the Corinthian church will be moved to report, 'God is truly
among you' (1 Cor. 14:25), both are saying something about
preaching that few today believe, let alone expect. Be honest,
do you?

Three features mark out Ezra as a reformed preacher in the
mould of any of the great Reformers of the sixteenth century.

Scripture alone

The first is his submission to the Word of God. Reformation

can be accomplished only by the application of the Bible's message to the hearts of men and women. *Sola Scriptura*, by Scripture alone, was his motto.

It is fascinating to note that it was the people who had asked for Ezra to come and expound the Scriptures to them (Neh. 8:1). They put themselves under the authority of God's Word. Nor was this easy, for their life-styles betrayed all the marks of having lived in Babylon. There were problems with marriage and divorce (see Ezra 9). Then the more tricky issue of personal finance: building was expensive and certain money-lenders in Jerusalem were prepared to allow their fellow Jews to mortgage their property, charging exorbitant interest. All this, in order to have the necessary money to buy bread (see Neh. 5).

And then there was worship. The Feast of Tabernacles had not been celebrated correctly for some 600 years and there was an urgent need for reformation in worship. Still the people desired to put themselves under the authority of the Bible (the 'Law of Moses, which the Lord had commanded Israel', Neh. 8:1), and Ezra, being the faithful preacher that he was, gladly used the opportunity to expound the Scriptures.

Built into Christianity is the principle of authority. God has made known to us his mind and will. He has revealed it in the Bible. The prime cause of the drift in the church today is a lack of commitment to this principle of authority. No one who knows his Bible can argue for the rightness of homosexuality, women in the ministry, or rock music as a form of worship.

Focus on Christ for a moment. He is on record as saying, 'I do nothing of myself; but as my Father taught me, I speak these things...for I always do those things that please him' (John 8:28-29; cf. 4:34; 5:30; 6:38; 8:26; 12:49-50; 14:31; 17:4). For Jesus, authority depended on his being subject to the Father. The knowledge that he was in the Father's will was to him a source of great strength. One day he rode into Jerusalem at the head of a cheering crowd. The next day, alone, he went through the temple like a hurricane, wrecking the bazaar in the Court of the Gentiles, throwing out the stallholders, upsetting the bankers' desks and puzzling onlookers with his display of fury at the business being transacted. Two big demonstrations of authority in two days! The next day the authorities gathered together to ask him outright: 'By what authority are you doing these things?' (Mark 11:28). His answer? His authority was from God.

Jesus claimed absolute authority about his teaching, 'You have heard that it was said... But I say to you' (Matt. 5:21-22) is one of many refrains. Add to this the following: 'Heaven and earth will pass away, but my words will by no means pass away' (Mark 13:31), and 'He who rejects me, and does not receive my words, has that which judges him — the word that I have spoken will judge him in the last day. For I have not spoken on my own authority; but the Father who sent me gave me a command, what I should say and what I should speak. And I know that his command is everlasting life. Therefore, whatever I speak, just as the Father has told me, so I speak' (John 12:48-50).

One of the areas of Jesus' teaching is crystal clear: over 200 references to the Old Testament in the Gospel records combine in vindicating his claim as to their absolute divine authority. Matters of doctrine (the resurrection, Mark 12:24-27), ethics (marriage, Matt. 19:5-6) and the wrongness of *corban* casuistry as a way out of one's obligations to the fifth commandment (Mark 7:10-13) were resolved by citing the Old Testament. Similarly Jesus conferred his authority upon the New Testament, promising the Spirit to help apostles write it (Mark 13:11; John 14:25-26; 15:26-27; 16:7-15; 20:21-23; Acts 1:8). And the apostles took it at face value making staggering claims like this one: 'We are of God. He who knows God hears us; he who is not of God does not hear us. By this we know the spirit of truth and the spirit of error' (1 John 4:6).

Thus Paul gives his parting counsel to his young son, colleague and friend Timothy to 'Preach the word' (2 Tim.

4:2). Which word? Paul has just told him, reminding him of former days when in his youth a godly mother and grandmother read to him from the Old Testament, God's inspired (breathed-out) Word which is able to make him (and us) wise for salvation through faith which is in Christ Jesus, and 'profitable for doctrine, for reproof, for correction, for instruction in righteousness, that the man of God may be complete, thoroughly equipped for every good work' (2 Tim. 3:15-17).

Little wonder seventeenth-century divines, reflecting on what was at the heart of Reformation preaching, began the *Westminster Confession of Faith* in this way: 'The whole counsel of God concerning all things necessary for his own glory, man's salvation, faith and life, is either expressly set down in Scripture, or by good and necessary consequence may be deduced from Scripture: unto which nothing at any time is to be added, whether by new revelations of the Spirit or traditions of men.'[1] We need to combat King Pragmatism, Lord Expediency and Prince Tradition by a firm belief in the authority of Scripture.

Explanation

'Do you understand what you are reading?' Philip asked the Ethiopian (Acts 8:30). Evidently he did not, and Philip had the joy of leading him to an appreciation of the fifty-third chapter of Isaiah that he had not known before. The Bible needs to be explained, for some things in it are not immediately clear, as even Peter remarked about some of Paul's writings (2 Peter 3:16).

This was the second feature of Ezra's preaching. We are told that he, along with a band of Levitical preachers, read the Word aloud to the people. A special pulpit of wood had been made for the occasion, but the focus of attention was not so much on Ezra as on the Word being expounded. 'So they read distinctly from the book, in the Law of God; and they gave the

sense, and helped them to understand the reading' (Neh. 8:8).
Three elements are worth noting: Ezra read the Word clearly,
followed it by exposition, and in such a way that his hearers
understood what God was saying to them. Such is what
preaching is all about. *It is letting the words of the Bible speak
for themselves.*

What do you look for in preaching? You must surely ask
yourself the question. A Christian, worth his salt, hears around
three sermons a week, 150 a year, around 10,000 in an average
life-time (based on Ps. 90:10). That's a lot of sermons! It
makes sense to ask ourselves what preaching is all about.
According to Ezra and his team, preaching is expounding
Scripture, bringing out of the text what is already there, prizing
open what appears closed, unravelling what seems to be
knotted, unfolding what seems tightly packed.

At the back of this kind of preaching lies the belief that
God speaks through his Word. The apostles confirm this by a
curious exchange of cryptic phrases when referring to the
Bible. Occasionally they would say, *gegraptai gar,* meaning
'it is written' (see Gal. 4:22). Whenever they do this they are
drawing attention to the authority of the Word. *Gegraptai gar*
was the end of any argument (see Jesus' threefold use of it
when knocking flat the devil's evil insinuations in Matthew
4:4,7,10). But occasionally the apostles spoke of Scripture as
continuing to speak, using *legei gar,* meaning 'it/he says' (a
present continuous tense). Both expressions assume that God
has spoken, but the latter goes on to suggest that God is
continuing to speak. Thus, in Hebrews 3 and 4, the author cites
from Psalm 95: 'Today, if you will hear his voice, do not
harden your hearts as in the rebellion,' introducing it by
saying, 'as the Holy Spirit says' (Heb. 3:7).

There are four ways in which God speaks in Psalm 95.
First, to Israelites in the wilderness, when God first spoke
these words but Israel hardened her heart. Second, the exhortation itself in Psalm 95 to Israel in David's own day. Third,
there was the exhortation to Christians in the first century A.D.

who were in danger of apostasy. Finally, there is the exhortation to us today as we continue to read the same words (and I venture to say any other age when Christians read the letter to the Hebrews).

There is a discipline involved in allowing the Bible to speak for itself. There is a similar discipline involved in allowing our ears to *hear* God speaking through the Bible's words.

Sermons: not for 'balconeers', but 'travellers'

A third area of Ezra's faithful preaching is the aim he had in view: he aimed at *reformation in the lives of God's people.*

Geoffrey Thomas makes a very telling point in a magnificent book called *Preaching.* It has to do with what folk expect when they listen to sermons. This is what he says: 'The most common criticism that is directed at our worship services is that apart from the hymns we sing, we ask people simply to be spectators. This is what drives them into charismatic meetings, where they are often hoodwinked into believing they have a larger part to play in the worship. The sermon should be the greatest period of participation in the church's assemblies. During a thirty-minute period a Christian should be moved to inward thankfulness and praise, conviction of sin and repentance, determination to love and obey God, new concern for his fellow-believers and his fellow men. The sermon is not for balconeers, but for travellers, for those who are most involved with God; it is the climactic aspect of worship. There is no more common cause of ineffective ministry than a failure in applicatory preaching.'[2]

Clearly, preaching *is* application. Ezra would concur heartily. Four immediate effects were forthcoming from his ministry. First, the congregation were *moved to worship* (Neh. 8:5-6). Second, they were *attentive to the sermon* (v. 3). Third, they were *obedient to its demands* (vv. 13-18). This needs a little explanation. During the course of the day's exposition on passages from Leviticus 23 they became aware that their worship had been sadly lacking in obedience in the matter of celebrating the Feast of Tabernacles. They clearly had been celebrating the festival itself, but ignoring the inconvenience of camping outside in rickety shelters! Immediately afterwards they went out and erected little shanties all over the city as a reminder of the days spent in such shanties in the wilderness.

Fourth, they *wept*. This was clearly the wrong reaction altogether. The law demanded that the Feast of Booths (Tabernacles) be an occasion for joy and merriment at the remembrance of the goodness of God shown to them (Deut. 16:15). Weeping was a proper response in worship for some occasions, but not this one. Nehemiah, Ezra's reforming companion, sends the people home to make merriment in the Lord. He does so by giving them one of the most wonderful texts in the Bible: 'The joy of the Lord is your strength' (Neh. 8:10).

It is, I think, easier to make people sad than joyful. Each of us resents being told to be happy when we have a mind to wallow in self-pity. There is nothing more irritating than Christian-Cheerful for whom life causes no problems and who doesn't understand that we do not share his buoyant euphoria.

We have swallowed the world's assessment of Christianity as a religion of doom and gloom too readily. Scripture bubbles with the opposite view: 'I will be glad and rejoice in you' (Ps. 9:2). 'You will show me the path of life; in your presence is fulness of joy; at your right hand are pleasures forevermore' (Ps. 16:11). 'You give them drink from the river of your pleasures' (Ps. 36:8). 'God, my exceeding joy' (Ps. 43:4). 'For the kingdom of God is... righteousness and peace and joy in the Holy Spirit' (Rom. 14:17). 'Now may the God of hope fill you with all joy and peace in believing...' (Rom. 15:13).

Isaac Watts was busily writing hymns well before the

Evangelical Awakening made him a household name in
Christian circles. One of his best-known hymns makes the
point we have been making above.

> Come we that love the Lord,
> And let our joys be known;
> Join in a song with sweet accord,
> And thus surround the throne.
>
> The sorrows of the mind
> Be banished from the place!
> Religion never was designed
> To make our pleasures less.
>
> Let those refuse to sing
> That never knew our God;
> But children of the heavenly King
> May speak their joys abroad.

A New England pastor, Dr Samuel West, threatened with a
strike from the choir over a long-standing quarrel, used this
very hymn to avert such a thing by asking the choir to lead the
singing beginning with the words, 'Let those refuse to sing
who never knew our God'!

Thus did God's people in Ezra's time experience the
power of God in their lives. Reformation came to Jerusalem.
Pray that we might experience one too!

8.
Doing what we can

Some of God's servants have only one talent: their usefulness is unlike that of Ezra's. They emerge as those who nevertheless 'do what they can'. One such was Mary of Bethany.

Jesus was in Bethany, some two miles from Jerusalem, dining with a man known as Simon the leper (perhaps because Jesus had healed him). There was a woman present who opened a jar containing expensive ointment and poured its contents on Jesus' head, in an act of anointing. The story is found in Mark 14: 3-9. John's version of the story gives us her name, Mary of Bethany, sister of Martha and Lazarus (John 12:1-8). No wonder she was thankful to Jesus after witnessing her brother's emergence from his grave after being dead for four days! (John 11:39).

A note of discord

How typical that it should have been Judas who objected as to the use of this ointment !(John 12:4-5). He had calculated it to be worth a year's wages. He could not tolerate whole-hearted devotion to Jesus, either in his own heart, or in others. Knowing nothing of grace in his own heart, Judas could not

comprehend Mary's depth of gratitude. For Judas this was just
a waste.

Ointment of this kind might well have been a family
heirloom, handed on from generation to generation. For this
woman the time for its use had come. She had reason to be
grateful to Jesus and wished to show it in some tangible way.
Some of those present protested at such extravagance. The
proceeds from the sale of this perfume could have been given
'to the poor' (v. 5). They were harsh in their criticism of her.
But Jesus describes her action as 'beautiful'.

This is a most moving story, so much so that Jesus tells his
guests that this woman's service to him should be remembered
'wherever this gospel is preached throughout the whole world'
(Mark 14:9). It is to be a 'memorial' of her love for Christ. It
is a wonderful testimony to leave behind, and it is salutary to
recall that this is not always the way. The Bible records, for
example, how Achan is remembered as the man whose sin
ruined the testimony of a whole nation (Josh. 7); and Lot's
wife was a memorial of that wistful longing after Sodom that
brought about her doom (Gen. 19). Mary of Bethany was to be
remembered by one thing: a whole-hearted, sacrificial and
earnest love for the Saviour. What an epitaph to leave behind:
'She loved Christ'!

Others too, have been quick to denounce Mary's action.
They have cited Jesus' concern for the poor: 'And whoever
gives one of these little ones only a cup of cold water in the
name of a disciple, assuredly, I say to you, he shall by no means
lose his reward' (Matt. 10:42). Or the words of James, 'Pure
and undefiled religion before God and the Father is this: to visit
orphans and widows in their trouble, and to keep oneself
unspotted from the world' (James 1:27).

How are we to reconcile Mary's action with these words?
The first thing to do is *not* to isolate one text of Scripture,
saying: 'This is the teaching of Scripture!' This is what the
cults do. They are forever taking a single text and saying in

effect that this is the entire teaching on this, or that, subject. All kinds of errors come this way. Instead, we must always be careful to take the text in the *context* of the portion of Scripture in which it is found, and then in relation to the teaching of the Bible in general. If we do that, it immediately becomes apparent that Jesus was not saying that concern for the poor was unimportant and unnecessary. Of course not! No one had shown such concern for the poor as he had. He had himself become poor! (2 Cor. 8:9).

'I love you'

This woman had appreciated something that the others hadn't. Jesus was not going to be with them for very much longer. Mark has made it quite clear as he retells the account in his Gospel that Jesus had forewarned the coming of his death on several occasions (8:31-2; 9:31; 10:33). If Mary of Bethany was to demonstrate her love for Jesus she must do so soon.

Have you, I wonder, ever thought that there is so little that you can offer to Christ in personal service? Your gifts seem so trivial in comparison to others. Perhaps your idea of usefulness, as I suggested at the very beginning of this book, is of someone like John Calvin, or John Wesley. This story about Mary of Bethany teaches us a very important lesson: no matter how insignificant we may appear to be there is always *something* that we can do for Jesus. No matter how little it may be, he sees it and acknowledges it.

O, what can little hearts do
To please the King of heaven?
Our hearts, if God his Spirit send,
Can love and trust their Saviour Friend:
Such grace to mine be given.

Though small is all that we can do
To please the King of heaven;
When hearts and hands and lips unite
To serve the Saviour with delight,
They're precious in his sight.

(Grace W. Hisdale).

Two Bible portraits illustrate this truth.

One is the story Jesus told about the widow's mite (Mark 12:41-44). Having finished teaching in the temple courts Jesus sat down near the area known as the Court of the Women where visitors to the temple gave their offerings. On the wall of the court were thirteen brass receptacles, in the shape of trumpets.[1] Every offering, if not seen, could easily be *heard*, and some would make considerable use of this facility in order to demonstrate the largeness of their offerings. After all, there were seats where people could observe, and hear, everything (v. 41).

Can you imagine, then, the tiny tinkling sound of a mite being dropped into one of these receptacles? No one present took any notice, apart, that is, from our Lord. He called his disciples over to take note of it. 'This poor widow has put in more than all those who have given to the treasury,' Jesus says (v. 43). This widow had given all that she had. That, in our Lord's reckoning, was greater than the largest tithe given that day. Even if a rich worshipper at the Passover had come and donated £500 (being a tenth of his income for that year) it did not compare to what this widow had done. *She had given everything.* Even small things can be of great service for God.

Sometimes we feel so useless for God. This is particularly so when we are unwell. Perhaps you are tempted to say, 'What can I possibly render to him?' It is at such times that Paul's instruction in 1 Corinthians 12 and Romans 12 is particularly helpful. Every part of the body is special. Every part has a function to perform.

John Milton, the seventeenth-century English poet, became blind. He felt useless and forgotten. His poem recalling the onset of blindness has some moving and instructive words which underline what we have just said:

When I consider how my light is spent
Ere half my days in this dark world and wide,
And that one talent which is death to hide
Lodged with me useless, though my soul more bent
To serve therewith my Maker, and present
My true account, lest returning chide,
'Doth God exact day-labour, light denied?'
I fondly ask. But Patience, to prevent
That murmur, soon replies, 'God doth not need
Either man's work or his own gifts. Who best
Bear his mild yoke, they serve him best. His state
Is kingly: thousands at his bidding speed,
And post o'er land and ocean without rest;
They also serve who only stand and wait.'

The other story which illustrates this same truth is the story of Onesimus. We all want to be useful for God. The mistake is to think that unless we are in the front line of battle (and publicity) we are somehow less useful. That's why the Bible gives us the example of Onesimus.

Onesimus was the runaway slave belonging to Philemon, an influential Christian at Colosse. He probably made Paul's acquaintance when Paul was a prisoner in Rome. He was converted through Paul's ministry (Philem. 10) and became a trustworthy brother to him (Col. 4:9).

Two features about Onesimus mark him out as particularly useful for God. The first is his name, Onesimus. This was a common name for a slave and it means useful. Slaves were often given this name not necessarily because they *were* useful but in the vague hope that the attachment of the name might act as an omen, and that they would *become* useful.

The second feature about Onesimus is something Paul says about him in his letter to his owner, Philemon. Having run away, Onesimus was liable under Roman law to be either tortured or punished by death (or both). Paul, who would have liked to have kept Onesimus, was obliged to return him to Philemon and urged his pardon and acceptance as a brother in the Lord: 'I appeal to you for my son Onesimus, whom I have begotten while in my chains, who once was unprofitable [useless] to you, but now is profitable [useful] to you and to me' (Philem. 10-11).

Knowing that his name means 'useful', or 'profitable', Paul makes a kind of joke about it, this time using another Greek word meaning 'useful' *(euchrestos)*. Before Onesimus' conversion he had been useless *(achrestos)*, but now he was really useful *(euchrestos)*. Not only is there a play on the word 'useful', but the very sound of the word *chrestos* is indistinguishable from that of the title Christ *(Christos)*. Before his conversion he had confirmed the general estimate of Phrygian slaves, that they were both unreliable and unfaithful. In Christ, however, it was altogether a different matter. A great change had taken place in this man's life. He had become both a Christian and useful! He was not a great preacher, or a missionary. He was a slave! Paul asked Philemon to pardon and release him so that he might be of help to the apostle. This is undoubtedly what happened.

Many slaves, however, who found their lives transformed by the gospel had owners who were not Christians. Paul urges these slaves to be obedient to their masters (Eph. 6:5-9). Obedience is the key that opens the door to usefulness. The seeds of happiness grow in the soil of obedience. Their lives might have lacked the excitement of some of God's great heroes of faith. Their names are now forgotten. Their accomplishments are nowhere recorded for posterity. But they were obedient in the task which God had set them; and they were useful for God.

Our lives may lack the excitement which the modern world often regards as essential. Mothers busily rearing young children, washing dirty clothes, ironing endless shirts, preparing meals that take hours to prepare and seem to be devoured in seconds can be forgiven for thinking that life isn't far short of Onesimus' slavery. But it would be a tragic mistake to think that they are not useful for God. Like Mary of Bethany, the widow and Onesimus found a usefulness in doing what they could for God.

A closer examination of the story of Mary anointing Jesus' head reveals many other lessons.

The personal touch

It was Jesus himself that Mary desired to honour. She wished to have direct and intimate dealings with Christ. In her silence Mary worshipped Christ. She had some inkling that soon he would die, but before he did so, she had this opportunity of showing him a little of her gratitude. She was totally absorbed by his presence. Her mind, her heart, her emotions, her will, were all fixed upon her Saviour. She saw and knew nothing else.

There is a lady who often reminds me, when the going is rough, 'See no one in the vision, but Christ.' It is good advice. Too often, our sight of Jesus is blurred. Faith is weak. The disciples had been challenged about their 'blurred vision' before, in Galilee. Jesus had just fed the great multitude creating a miraculous supply of food from a few loaves and fishes (Mark 8:1-10). It had been a wonderful sign of the greatness of his power. Jesus really was King!

Afterwards, in a boat on the Sea of Galilee the disciples were upset — they had forgotten to bring bread! They were frustrated and Jesus warned them of the 'yeast' of the Pharisees.

How quickly their hearts were filled with unbelief after witnessing such a great miracle!

Immediately afterwards Jesus underlined the point by a curious incident involving the healing of a blind man (Mark 8:22-26). What is unusual about this story is that his healing was, initially, incomplete. After Jesus had spat upon his eyes he asked him what he could see. 'I see men like trees, walking,' he said (v. 24). When Jesus placed his hands on him a second time, he saw 'everyone clearly' (v. 25). What was Jesus saying in this incident? It was simply this: that their vision of him was blurred. They were far too caught up with themselves to see him.

This is the question to challenge all of us: 'How much of Christ fills our vision from day to day?' In our praying and reading of the Scriptures, are we conscious of his presence? Are we mindful of the glory and power of his person as we draw near to him? This is what Christianity is all about. It was Luther who said that Christianity was all to do with personal pronouns, by which he meant that one must be able to say, 'The Lord is *my* Shepherd! He gave himself for *me*! I know that *my* Redeemer lives! He loves *me*!' The point we need to grasp and apply to our hearts is this: has our faith become academic? Has the freshness of personal dealings with Christ grown stale and formal?

Mary sat at Jesus' feet, getting everything into proportion. In contrast to Mary, her sister Martha was the practical type, managing one of the most distinguished homes in the village of Bethany, where Jesus on more than one occasion had received hospitality. Mary, on the other hand, was preoccupied with the one before her, anointing his head and feet with precious ointment (cf. Luke 10:38-39).

The Puritan John Owen had this to say about the value of meditating on Christ: 'He that looks steadily on the sun, although he cannot bear the lustre of its beams fully, yet his sight is so affected with it that when he calls off his eyes from it, he can see nothing as it were of the things about him; they are all dark unto him. And he who looks steadily in his contemplations on things above, eternal things, though he cannot comprehend their glory, yet a veil will be cast by it on all the desirable beauties of earthly things, and take off his affections from them.'[2]

My best for him

Mary gave the most precious thing she had to her Saviour. What a lesson that is for us! She could quite easily have bought some oil from the bazaar in Bethany at little cost (olive oil was plentiful). Instead she took of her treasure, perhaps as we have suggested, an heirloom, and donated it for the Lord's service.

Jesus deserves from us the same kind of service. If you teach in Sunday school then he deserves the best in preparation for the lessons. The children deserve the best love and attention that can be given to them. Office-bearers in the church must devote the best care and attention over Christ's flock. Jesus deserves better than the 'scrag-ends' of our time. The best hours should be given to prayer and Scripture reading. And Jesus himself urges us to keep the best emotions and reserve them for him, for anyone who loves someone else more than Jesus is not worthy of him (Mark 10:29-30).

There is to be no 'holding-back' in God's service. Grudging workers are poor workers.

A sign of things to come

Our Lord commented that Mary's service that day had foreshadowed an event shortly to come to pass in Jesus' life. 'She has come beforehand to anoint my body for burial' (Mark 14:8).

This had been no spur of the moment action on Mary's part. It shows all the hallmarks of premeditation. She may even have planned it many months in advance. If she hadn't herself heard him speak of his departure, she would have heard others do so (cf.Mark 8:31-2; 9:31; 10:33). No doubt, she had meditated upon the significance of Christ's coming. He had come to die for his people. To die as her Saviour! As her substitute he would have to suffer the cruel death of a Roman execution. Perhaps some of the words of the prophet Isaiah had come rushing back to her: 'This is the Lord's Servant' she might have said to herself (cf. Isa. 42:1-4). This is that tender plant, that root out of a dry ground. This is the one who must suffer the rejection of men. This is the man of sorrows who is acquainted with grief. It is he who bears our grief and carries our sorrows. He it is who will be smitten by God, afflicted, and bruised for our iniquities (cf. Isa. 53).

In breaking the flask (Mark 14:3), an Aramaic custom signifying that the purpose for its existence was now served, she began to smear the ointment on Jesus' head and feet. It was a faith that showed itself in service for God. There was an obedience of faith (Rom. 1:5), a work of faith (1 Thess. 1:3). She did not plan to let the event slip by and find the work left undone. It was Passover and it was time for action. Mary stands as a monument, not only of good intentions, but of deeds done.

Silence!

Mary never said a word! Hers was not the idle, gossiping tongue. Someone has said of Mary that she will have a short time giving an account of every idle word on the Day of Judgement! (Matt. 12:36). As Moody Stuart records of her, 'In Martha's house Mary listens, and is silent; at her brother's grave she weeps, and is silent; in the house of Simon she works, and is silent. She speaks not, that she may hear, that she may weep, that she may work. What a blessing it would be to the church and the world, if Christian women would think of

Mary; if they would learn from her this one lesson of being "swift to hear, and slow to speak".[3]

Mary wasn't concerned about the applause of others. She did it for her Lord. It was his approval she sought. Happy is the one who sits beside her, at Jesus' feet, happy in serving him.

O love divine, how sweet thou art!
When shall I find my willing heart
All taken up by thee?
I thirst, I faint, I die to prove
The greatness of redeeming love,
The love of Christ to me.

Stronger his love than death or hell;
Its riches are unsearchable;
The first-born sons of light
Desire in vain its depths to see;
They cannot reach the mystery,
The length, and breadth, and height.

God only knows the love of God;
O that it now were shed abroad
In this poor stony heart!
For love I sigh, for love I pine;
This only portion, Lord, be mine,
Be mine this better part!

O, that I could for ever sit
With Mary at the Master's feet!
Be this my happy choice.
My only care, delight and bliss
My joy, my heaven on earth, be this
To hear the Bridegroom's voice.

(Charles Wesley).

9.
Useful at last!

Jesus was dead. The previous twenty-four hours in Jerusalem had seen nothing like it. None had witnessed such a Passover week as this one. Jesus, the preacher from Galilee, had been betrayed, tried and executed as a common criminal. And now, mid-afternoon on the Friday of Passover week, Jesus was dead. There were only a few hours of sunlight left before the onset of the Jewish Sabbath, and if Jesus was to be buried it had to be arranged quickly. It is here that Joseph of Arimathea makes his courageous entrance to usefulness.

Some Christians seem to be raised up for just one supreme work of usefulness in God's kingdom. The rest of their lives seem to be a preparation for one, brief act of service for the Lord. It was to be just so for Joseph. This was to be the moment of opportunity. And he was ready for it.

'The plain truth is that many believers in the present day feel so dreadfully afraid of doing harm that they hardly ever dare to do good. There are many who are fruitful in objections, but barren in actions; rich in wet-blankets, but poor in anything like Christian fire... Truly, in looking round the Church of Christ, a man might sometimes think that God's kingdom has come, and God's will was being done on earth, so small is the zeal that some believers show. It is vain to deny it.'[1] That was J.C.Ryle's view of Victorian Christianity, and it might as well

have been written yesterday for very little has changed. There
are few that could be accused of being 'mad' in their zeal for
the kingdom of God as Paul was by Festus (Acts 26:24).
Zealous, however, is what we are meant to be: '[Christ] gave
himself for us, that he might redeem us from every lawless
deed and purify for himself his own special people, zealous for
good works' (Titus 2:14). It was the problem with the church
at Laodicea that caused such a sense of revulsion in God, that
she was 'lukewarm' and needed to be 'zealous and repent'
(Rev. 3:15,16,19).

   In our brief study of some of God's workers we have seen
giants like Joseph and Ezra. We have also seen those, like
Mary of Bethany, whose gifts are substantially less, yet used
for Christian service. There are also those who are shy and
diffident about their gifts. They are reticent to come forward
and show themselves willing. Like Joseph of Arimathea, they
lack zeal for God, they are 'secret disciples' — until, that is,
God needs them the most. Then they show themselves as true
disciples, bold for the Master's use.

Emerging from the shadows

Joseph was a good and righteous man...and he was looking for
the kingdom of God (Luke 23:50-51). He was a member of the
Sanhedrin which had condemned Jesus to death, but Scripture
informs us, without explanation, that he had been absent. He
was a disciple of Jesus, but secretly, because he feared the
reaction of the Jews if he were openly to confess his allegiance
(John 19:38). Nor was he the only one: 'Among the chief rulers
also many believed on him, but because of the Pharisees they
did not confess him, lest they should be put out of the
synagogue' (John 12:42).

   There are a host of reasons why a person should be a secret
disciple. First, there is *personality*. A man's character is
something very unique. It is a most remarkable thing that each

person is different from the other. No two are just alike. Even within a single family it is quite astonishing to note that children of the same parents can be so utterly different in their personalities. One is extrovert and out-going. Another is shy and retiring. One is naturally confident and enthusiastic. Another is diffident and unsure of himself. One is ebullient and another is melancholic and broody. Sometimes a single person can demonstrate a variety of personality traits. He can even have what we sometimes call a 'split personality'. In schizophrenia this can become a marked problem.

Even in the process of inspiration whereby 'holy men of God spoke as they were moved by the Holy Spirit' (2 Peter 1:21), the individual personalities of the writers come through. Take the Gospels: there is a world of difference between Mark's Gospel and that of John. It is the same with the prophets: Isaiah, or Amos, or Jeremiah, or Nahum. After a while a Christian familiar with his Bible can get the feel of an individual style and will be able to say, 'It must be Isaiah!'

We must not despise Joseph's retiring character. The man who is always opening his mouth is not necessarily a good witness. Spurgeon speaks of those who are 'fearless because they are brainless'!

Second, there is variety in *Christian experience*. The experience of conversion can vary enormously. Timothy was converted as a child and his experience was quite different to that of Paul. Take Bishop Ryle's testimony: 'The circumstances which led to a complete change in my character were many and very various, and I think it right to mention them. It was not a sudden immediate change but very gradual. I cannot trace it to any one person, or any one event or thing, but to a singular variety of persons and things. In all of them I believe now the Holy Ghost was working, though I did not know it at the time.'[2]

Then take as another example the testimony of Hudson Taylor, founder of the China Inland Mission: 'On a day which I shall never forget, when I was about fifteen years of age, my dear mother being absent from home, I had a holiday, and in the afternoon looked through my father's library to find some book with which to while away the unoccupied hours. Nothing attracted me, I turned over a little basket of pamphlets, and selected from amongst them a gospel tract which looked interesting, saying to myself, "There will be a story at the commencement, and a sermon or moral at the close: I will take the former and leave the latter for those who like it."

'I sat down to read the little book in an utterly unconcerned state of mind, believing indeed at the time that if there were any salvation it was not for me... Little did I know at the time what was going on in the heart of my dear mother, seventy or eighty miles away. She rose from the dinner-table that afternoon with an intense yearning for the conversion of her boy, and feeling that — absent from home, and having more leisure than she could otherwise secure — a special opportunity was afforded her of pleading with God on my behalf. She went to her room and turned the key in the door, resolved not to leave that spot until her prayers were answered. Hour after hour did that mother plead for me, until at length she could pray no longer, but was constrained to praise God for that which his Spirit taught her had already been accomplished — the conversion of her only son.

'I in the meantime had been led in the way I have mentioned to take up this little tract, and while reading it was struck with the sentence, "The finished work of Christ". The thought passed through my mind, "Why does the author use this expression? ...What was finished?" And I at once replied, "A full and perfect atonement and satisfaction for sin: the debt was paid by the Substitute; Christ died for our sins, and not for ours only but also for the sins of the whole world." Then came the thought, "If the whole work was finished and the whole debt paid, what is there left for me to do?" And with this dawned the joyful conviction, as light was flashed into my soul by the Holy Spirit, that there was nothing in the world to be done but to fall down on one's knees, and accepting this

Saviour and his salvation, to praise him for evermore. Thus while my dear mother was praising God on her knees in her chamber, I was praising him in the old warehouse to which I had gone alone to read at my leisure this little book.'[3]

'Stand up and be counted'

These two accounts of spiritual conversion are very different, yet their end result (repentance and faith in Jesus Christ) is the same.

It does not follow, however, that an undramatic conversion experience results in a Christian who lacks zeal and fire, any more than that the contrary is true. Ryle's experience was singularly undramatic, but who would accuse him of being a secret disciple — any more than Timothy, whose experience was something similiar, yet whose life was one of zealous devotion to the Lord's service? Yet, because of the fact that *in some* the assurance of salvation (their self-awareness of the Spirit-given spiritual life within their hearts) develops slowly and gradually, together with the fact that their experience of conversion is undramatic, this, *in some*, only further encourages the secretiveness of their resultant Christian testimony.

There is, however, a third factor which must be taken into consideration here. For even though Joseph's timidity owed much to both his personality and the nature of his conversion they do not totally explain it. Scripture records the one essential factor in the understanding of his diffidence: *he feared the Jews* (John 19:38). Joseph was a wealthy man and a member of the Sanhedrin court. He had a position of respect and power in society. They were all put at considerable risk by a public allegiance to Christ. Little wonder he was afraid!

But no one can remain a secret follower of Jesus for ever. Sooner or later a crisis comes where we must 'stand up and be counted'. And once you make that stand there is no going back.

Just as Julius Caesar is supposed to have said 'The die is cast,' before crossing the River Rubicon, so Joseph could say it now.

Whatever aspects of Joseph's character excuse his diffidence, the time had now come for bold, assertive action. Joseph became useful at last! The presence of the Holy Spirit within a person's heart can effect a most radical change in that person's character. It would seem that something of this sort happened in the case of Joseph. The Holy Spirit working in his heart produced a transformation of character so that now he was ready to stand up and be counted, no matter what the cost to himself. We must not limit the Spirit's power to change us, nor must we ever excuse our sin by insisting it is some ineradicable aspect of our personality.

> Am I a soldier of the cross
> A follower of the Lamb
> And shall I fear to own his cause
> Or blush to speak his name?
>
> Must I be carried to the skies
> On flowery beds of ease
> While others fought to win the prize
> And sail'd through bloody seas?

(Isaac Watts).

The final evening

It was Friday evening and the Sabbath was imminent. Jerusalem's population, normally around 50,000, was now swelled to about 200,000 by the Passover celebrations. Yet there had never been a Passover like this one. Something had happened that day to cause stout-hearted men to tremble. Jesus of Nazareth had been crucified.

He had entered triumphantly with people shouting and singing and throwing down palm leaves in his way. But he had been betrayed — by one of his own. On Thursday evening, in the Garden of Gethsemane, soldiers had come and taken him away.

All this Jesus had foretold when eating the Passover with his disciples in an upper room in John Mark's house. After singing the final psalm they had gone through one of the city gates, across the Kidron valley and to the foot of the Mount of Olives. On the way he had cited from Zechariah: 'I will strike the Shepherd, and the sheep of the flock will be scattered' (Zech. 13:7). Then he had added something even more strange: 'After I have been raised, I will go before you to Galilee' (Matt. 26:31,32). The disciples, Peter especially, had protested they would never desert him.

He had entered the Garden of Gethsemane, kindly lent to him by John Mark's father. Surrounded by walls to keep out thieves, it was an ideal place for solitude. Jesus was praying when the knocking was heard at the door and men with torches and weapons entered. Peter, James and John had been half asleep, but were now wide enough awake to see Judas leading the high priest's motley band and pointing out Jesus to them — with a kiss! Peter had one of his moments of rage and boldness, and swiftly took a sword and struck off the ear of a slave called Malchus. Jesus restored the ear — it was to be his final public miracle. And then he surrendered to these men, demanding the release of his disciples, who promptly fled. Mark had come, awakened by the noise, a sheet wrapped around him which he lost in the ensuing struggle, fleeing naked from the garden.

There had been a trial — all very hastily and improperly conducted. Annas, Caiaphas, even Pilate had been involved. John knew the high priest and his servants and had managed to gain access for himself and Peter. They had heard their Lord's affirmative response to Caiaphas' question: 'Are you the Christ, the Son of the Blessed?' There had also been a state trial before Pilate. The Sanhedrin had met early on the Friday morning and quickly decided that Jesus ought to be put to death. They had no such power, but Pilate was such a weak, vacillating man that what the Sanhedrin lacked in power Pilate abundantly supplied. Normally he would not have been there in Jerusalem, but it was Passover time and he was to be found in the Fortress of Antonia at the north-west corner of the temple.

He had found no fault in Christ. He had even told the Sanhedrin to go and crucify Jesus themselves because he had no desire to do so. But, being afraid of what Caesar might say if there should be any trouble, and the reaction of the crowd if he should fail to comply with their hysterical cries to have Jesus crucified, he complied with the request. He had first offered to release him as a token of his favour to the Jews on the eve of Passover, but the crowd had asked for a certain Barabbas to be released instead.

Pilate had Jesus scourged before letting him go. It was a cruel and spiteful thing to have done. His flesh had been lacerated, exposing veins and arteries, but it had not killed him as it had done some. Soldiers had taken him away to the Praetorium where they mocked him and even spat in his face. Then they led him away to Golgotha to be crucified. Simon of Cyrene had helped him carry the beam laid across his back. Nails were driven into his hands and feet and the cross being lifted up was jerked into a hole in the ground. There he was left, interrupted only by the jeering of the chief priests and the offer of vinegar to drink.

There was one terrible moment in it all when the whole of Jerusalem became black as night and Jesus was heard to cry, *'Eloi, Eloi, lama sabachthani?'* (which means 'My God, my God, why have you forsaken me?'). The curtain in the temple had ripped in half and according to Matthew, tombs nearby evidenced a resurrection of certain people who had died and had been buried there. And the centurion who had stood guard by the cross was heard to mutter, 'Truly this was the Son of God!' (Matt. 27:50-54).

The Rubicon

Now Jesus was dead. There was no doubt about it, a spear had been thrust into his side to make sure. He had stopped breathing and all life had ceased. He was dead, and it was only a few hours before the onset of Sabbath. There was no time for a proper burial. At the cross only a few had remained to the end: Mary Magdalene, the 'other' Mary (Clopas' wife), Joanna, Susanna, Nicodemus and Joseph of Arimathea. What a day it had been for them! Surely, every detail of it was etched on their minds as they stood in awe and wonder before the one they had known as Jesus of Nazareth.

This was the moment Joseph was to show his usefulness. It was the crossing of the Rubicon. 'The die was cast.' He went to visit Pilate after it became certain that Jesus had died. He was by now willing to suffer any ridicule in order to have Jesus decently buried. After gaining Pilate's permission for the body to be handed over to his custody, he went to consult with Nicodemus and the women as to what to do in so short a time, for darkness and the Jewish Sabbath were fast approaching. Ordinarily the body would have been washed, anointed with perfume and dressed in clean outer garments. There was no time for any of that. Instead, Joseph bought a large linen cloth from the market while Nicodemus obtained a large supply of dry spices (five stone of it — enough for a king!) to pack around the body as a temporary anti-putrefactant. The cloth, a large sheet, was wrapped around the body, bandages being used to hold the feet, hands and chin in place. It was all done in a great hurry; there was no time to wash the body or dress it in any way.

Joseph was God's provision in a time of need. He always provides when there is a need. The disciples had fled in fear. Jerusalem was volatile, and there were enemies of Christ everywhere and it is too distressing even to contemplate what might have happened if Joseph, this shy, timid man, had not intervened so magnanimously.

What moved this man to give up his own tomb, to go before Pilate and plead for Jesus' body, to organize so effectively Christ's burial? What caused him to be out-and-out for Christ, to be wholly on the Lord's side? Like Caleb before him, he could now be said to be serving the Lord whole-heartedly (Num.14:24; 32:12; Deut.1:36; Josh. 14:8,9,14).

An understanding of the cross had affected him! After witnessing the crucifixion, and hearing Jesus' own explanation of it, Joseph had become aware that as a believer he too must be prepared to sacrifice his life for him.

Saviour, Thy dying love Thou gavest me,
Nor should I aught withhold, dear Lord, from Thee:
In love my soul would bow, my heart fulfil its vow,
Some off'ring bring Thee now, something for Thee.

Give me a faithful heart, guided by Thee,
That each departing day henceforth may see
Some work of love begun, some deed of kindness done,
Some wand'rer sought and won, something for Thee.

Those words were written by Sylvanus Dryden Phelps, an American Baptist minister in 1862. Of all that Phelps accomplished for Christ in his life, he is remembered by this one hymn. The accompanying music 'Something for Jesus' was written by Robert Lowry, who on the occasion of Phelps' seventieth birthday sent a telegram, saying: 'It is worth living seventy years, even if nothing comes of it but one such hymn as this one. Happy is the man who can produce one song which the world will keep on singing after its author shall have passed away.'[4]

Doing 'something for Jesus', even if it is only one thing, is useful. *Let us be useful for God!*

References

Chapter 1

1. T. H. L.Parker, *John Calvin* (Westminster Press, 1975), pp.151-152.
2. Cited in S.M.Houghton, *Sketches From Church History* (Banner of Truth, 1980), p.192.
3. *The Journals of Jim Elliot* (Pickering and Inglis, 1978), p.401.
4. *The Parables of Jesus* (Inter-Varsity Press, 1989), p.117.
5. C. H. Spurgeon, *Lectures To My Students* (Marshall Morgan & Scott, 1970), p.26. Though Spurgeon possibly goes too far in his stress on the need for a 'felt desire' saying in effect that if a man can do anything else, he should, the overall point is valid.
6. See *The Spirit of Promise*, by Donald Macleod (Christian Focus Publications, 1986), chapter 5.

Chapter 2

1. John Waters, *Storming the Golden Kingdom*, (IVP/STL, 1989), p. 29.

Chapter 3

1. Thomas Brooks, *Precious Remedies Against Satan's Devices* (Banner of Truth, 1984), p.151.
2. Sinclair Ferguson, *Daniel*, The Communicator's Commentary (Word Books, 1989), pp.28-29.
3. *Westminster Confession of Faith*, Chapter 5, sections i, iv, ii and v respectively.

Chapter 4

1. Rudolph Otto, *The Idea of the Holy* (Oxford University Press, 1923), p.25.
2. Martyn Lloyd-Jones, *Romans, An Exposition of Chapter 6: The New Man* (Banner of Truth, 1972), p.144.
3. A. W. Tozer, *The Set of the Sail* (Kingsway Publications, 1986), p.35.

Chapter 5

1. John Calvin, *Commentaries on the Epistles to Timothy, Titus, and Philemon* (Baker, 1981), p.231.
2. Thomas Brooks, *Collected Works*, vol. 5 (Banner of Truth, 1980), p.4.
3. John Owen, *The Works of John Owen*, vol. 6 (Banner of Truth, 1974).
4. As above, p.22.
5. As above, p.23.
6. As above, p.30.
7. For a penetrating analysis, see J.I.Packer, *Laid Back Religion?* (IVP, 1989), chapter 4: 'Hot Tub Religion: Towards a Theology of Pleasure.'
8. Elliot, *Journals*, p. 475.

Chapter 6

1. Gaius Davies, *Stress, the Challenge to Christian Caring* (Kingsway Publications, 1988), p.46.
2. As above, p.28.
3. Sinclair B. Ferguson, *Man Overboard! The Story of Jonah* (Pickering and Inglis, 1981), p.101.
4. C. S. Lewis, *The Screwtape Letters* (Fontana Books, 1959), p.9.
5. William Gurnall, *The Christian in Complete Armour* (Banner of Truth, 1964). See also the modernized abridgement also published in three volumes by the Banner of Truth Trust.
6. See C. H. Spurgeon, *An Autobiography, The Early Years* (Banner of Truth, 1973), pp.427-451.

Chapter 7

1. *Westminster Confession of Faith*, Chapter 1, section vi.
2. *Preaching*, ed. Samuel T. Logan. Essay entitled, 'Powerful Preaching' by Geoffrey Thomas (Evangelical Press, 1986), p.380.

Chapter 8

1. See William Lane, *The Gospel of Mark* (Marshall, Morgan & Scott, 1974), p.442.
2. John Owen, *Works*, Vol. 7, section entitled "The Grace and Duty of being Spiritually Minded" (Banner of Truth, 1965), p.318.
3. A. Moody Stuart, *The Three Marys* (Banner of Truth, 1984), p.192.

Chapter 9

1. J. C. Ryle, *Practical Religion* (James Clarke, 1970),
    p.145.
2. J. C. Ryle, *A Self Portrait* (Reiner Publications, 1975),
    pp.38-39.
3. Marshall Broomhall, *Hudson Taylor, The man who
    believed God* (The Religious Tract Society, 1930),
    pp.24-25.
4. Helen Salem Rizk, *Stories of the Christian Hymns*
    (Hodder and Stoughton, 1966) p.49.

More books from
EVANGELICAL PRESS

HOW TO SHARE YOUR FAITH
Leith Samuel

David Jackman writes in his foreword: 'Here are plenty of helpful advice and priority principles about how we can better show our faith in contemporary society.

'But its greatest value is that in being provided with such valuable material, we are also led closer to Christ and deepened in our love and devotion to him.'
Paperback, 116 pages.
ISBN 0 85234 208 X.

HOW TO KNOW GOD'S WILL
Derek Cleave

The most important thing in anyone's life is to know the will of God and to follow it. So how are we to know God's purpose for our lives? Is there some formula we can apply to get the answer? The author clearly shows us what we must do to find God's will.
Paperback, 90 pages.
ISBN 0 85234 200 4.
'Full of practical "sanctified" common sense! He is able to draw on his wide experience as both pastor and evangelist to well illustrate these themes.'

A MAN AND HIS GOD
The Christian and the life of faith
Denis Lane

'If only I had more faith!' is a cry from the heart of many Christians. True faith is a living link with God that affects every area of our life. Such faith is clearly exemplified in the life of Abraham. Here we see what the true relationship should be between 'a man and his God'.
Paperback, 160 pages.
ISBN 0 85234 155 5.

'The message of the book is vital - it aims to clarify the average Christian's concept of faith and stimulate new confidence in the eternal God. It shows him as the focus of our faith, the anchor of the ship - the rock of foundation.'

Christian Herald

EVERYDAY EVANGELISM
Gareth Crossley

'The church today can no longer assume the right to speak to the unsaved about the great issues of life and death. We have to earn that right.'
The author believes that the approach of the Christian church to the unsaved has often been highly stereotyped and that we need to take a fresh look at the great principles of evangelism outlined in the Scriptures. He examines the question of evangelism, the need to mobilize the church (all its members!), the place and importance of evangelists, strategy, persistence, flexibility, social concern and church growth. Handle with care-this book is designed to produce action!
Paperback, 249 pages.
ISBN 0 85234 239 X.

THROUGH MANY DANGERS
The story of John Newton
Brian Edwards

An exciting and compelling story of one of the great heroes of the Christian faith. A common sailor at the age of eleven and press-ganged onto a man-of-war at nineteen, John Newton experienced the thrill of action against French warships, the cruel lash of navy discipline for desertion, the loose and blasphemous life of a free thinker and the pain of an overwhelming love for a girl beyond his reach. This story of the author of the hymn 'Amazing Grace' will warm every Christian heart and intrigue those who normally have little time for religion.

Paperback, 200 pages.
ISBN 0 85234 141 5.

'Gripping to read, it is informative, challenging and calculated to be a blessing to the soul.'

Grace Magazine

LUKE COMES ALIVE
John Blanchard

Popular writer and evangelist John Blanchard presents two months' daily Bible readings, taking the reader through the Gospel of Luke.

Both informative and challenging, the author's lively style will make this book of great help to readers in their everyday life and enhance their understanding of the Scriptures.

Paperback, 128 pages.
ISBN 0 85234 223 3.

HOW TO ENJOY YOUR BIBLE

John Blanchard

Reading the Scriptures should be an exciting adventure into God's truth and purposes for our lives. So how can we enjoy God's Word and avoid the trap of our Bible study being a dull, boring duty? In this excellent book, the author, an internationally-known preacher and evangelist, shows us how this can be achieved, giving all who read it a fresh desire to study and enjoy God's Word, the Bible.

Paperback, 159 pages.
ISBN 0 85234 182 2.

'Simple, vivid, accurate, warm, practical and searching, it is all that we have come to expect of its author.'

J.I.Packer